Crime
and the
American Press

PRAEGER SERIES IN POLITICAL COMMUNICATION
Robert E. Denton, Jr., General Editor

Crime and the American Press

Roy Edward Lotz

Praeger Series in Political Communication

New York
Westport, Connecticut
London

Library of Congress Cataloging-in-Publication Data

Lotz, Roy, 1943–
    Crime and the American press / Roy Edward Lotz.
       p.   cm. — (Praeger series in political communication)
    Includes bibliographical references and index.
    ISBN 0–275–94012–8 (alk. paper)
    1. Crime and the press—United States. 2. Investigative
reporting—United States. 3. Newspaper court reporting—United
States. 4. Journalism, Legal—United States.   I. Title.
II. Series.
PN4888.C8L67   1991
070.4'49364'0973—dc20   91–4623

British Library Cataloguing in Publication Data is available.

Library of Congress Catalog Card Number: 91–4623
ISBN: 0–275–94012–8

First published in 1991

Praeger Publishers, One Madison Avenue, New York, NY 10010
An imprint of Greenwood Publishing Group, Inc.

Printed in the United States of America

The paper used in this book complies with the
Permanent Paper Standard issued by the National
Information Standards Organization (Z39.48–1984).

10 9 8 7 6 5 4 3 2 1

To Bernard Rosenberg,
a friend, scholar, and,
as my father would have put it,
a good egg

Contents

About the Series

Those of us from the discipline of communication studies have long believed that communication is prior to all other fields of inquiry. In several other forums I have argued that the essence of politics is "talk" or human interaction.[1] Such interaction may be formal or informal, verbal or nonverbal, public or private, but always persuasive, forcing us consciously or subconsciously to interpret, to evaluate, and to act. Communication is the vehicle for human action.

From this perspective, it is not surprising that Aristotle recognized the natural kinship of politics and communication in his writings of *Politics* and *Rhetoric*. In the former, he establishes that humans are "political beings [who] alone of the animals [are] furnished with the faculty of language."[2] And in the latter, he begins his systematic analysis of discourse by proclaiming that "rhetorical study, in its strict sense, is concerned with the modes of persuasion."[3] Thus, it was recognized over 2,000 years ago that politics and communication go hand in hand because they are essential parts of human nature.

Back in 1981, Dan Nimmo and Keith Sanders proclaimed that political communication was an emerging field.[4] Although its origin, as noted, dates back centuries, a self-consciously cross-disciplinary focus began in the late 1950s. Thousands of books and articles later, colleges and universities offer a variety of graduate and undergraduate coursework in the area, in such diverse departments as communication, mass communication, journalism, political science, and sociology.[5] In Nimmo and Sanders's early assessment, the "key areas of inquiry" included rhetorical analysis, propaganda analysis, attitude change studies, voting studies, government and the news media, functional and systems analyses, technological changes, media technologies, campaign techniques, and research techniques.[6] In a survey about the field conducted by the same authors and Lynda Kaid in 1983, they found additional, more specific areas of concern such as the presidency, political polls, public opinion, debates, and advertising, to name a few.[7] They also noted a shift since the first study away from the rather strict behavioral approach.

Today Dan Nimmo and David Swanson assert that "political communication has developed some identity as a more or less distinct domain of scholarly work."[8] The scope and concerns of the area have further expanded to include critical theories and cultural studies. While there is no precise definition, method, or disciplinary home for this area of inquiry, its primary domain is the role, processes, and effects of communication within the context of politics broadly defined.

In 1985, the editors of *Political Communication Yearbook: 1984* noted that "more things are happening in the study, teaching, and practice of political communication than can be captured within the space limitations of the relatively few publications available."[9] In addition, they argued that the backgrounds of "those involved in the field [are] so varied and pluralist in outlook and approach, . . . it [is] a mistake to adhere slavishly to any set format in shaping the content."[10] And more recently, Swanson and Nimmo called for "ways of overcoming the unhappy consequences of fragmentation within a framework that respects, encourages, and benefits from diverse scholarly commitments, agendas, and approaches."[11]

In agreement with these assessments of the area and with gentle encouragement, Praeger established in 1988 the series entitled "Praeger Studies in Political Communication." This series is open to all qualitative and quantitative methodologies and to contemporary and historical studies. The studies in the series focus on communication variables or activities within a political context or dimension. Scholars from the disciplines of communication, history, political science, and sociology have participated in the series.

I am, without shame or modesty, a fan of the series. The joy of serving as its editor is in participating in the dialogue of the field of political communication and in reading the contributors' works. I invite you to join me.

Robert E. Denton, Jr.

NOTES

1. See Robert E. Denton, Jr., *The Symbolic Dimensions of the American Presidency* (Prospect Heights, IL: Waveland Press, 1982); Robert E. Denton, Jr., and Gary Woodward, *Political Communication in America* (New York: Praeger, 1985, 2nd

ed., 1990); Robert E. Denton, Jr., and Dan Hahn, *Presidential Communication* (New York: Praeger, 1986); Robert E. Denton, Jr., *The Primetime Presidency of Ronald Reagan* (New York: Praeger, 1988).

2. Aristotle, *The Politics of Aristotle*, trans. Ernest Barker (New York: Oxford University Press, 1970), p. 5.

3. Aristotle, *Rhetoric*, trans. Rhys Roberts (New York: The Modern Library, 1954), p. 22.

4. Dan Nimmo and Keith Sanders, "Introduction: The Emergence of Political Communication as a Field," in *Handbook of Political Communication*, ed. Dan Nimmo and Keith Sanders (Beverly Hills, CA: Sage, 1981), pp. 11–36.

5. Ibid., p. 15.

6. Ibid., pp. 17–27.

7. Keith Sanders, Lynda Kaid, and Dan Nimmo, eds., *Political Communication Yearbook, 1984* (Carbondale: Southern Illinois University: 1985), pp. 283–308.

8. Dan Nimmo and David Swanson, "The Field of Political Communication: Beyond the Voter Persuasion Paradigm" in *New Directions in Political Communication*, ed. David Swanson and Dan Nimmo (Beverly Hills, CA: Sage, 1990), p. 8.

9. Sanders, Kaid, and Nimmo, p. xiv.

10. Ibid.

11. Nimmo and Swanson, p. 11.

Series Foreword

There is growing debate about the role and function of the press in America. At the birth of our nation, journalists were singled out as essential to democracy with the First Amendment of the Bill of Rights protecting the freedom of the press. As our nation has grown, so too have the power, influence, and importance of the press. While it is true that the media do not tell us what to think, they do influence what we think about. It seems that the media, rather than our leaders, tell us what is important, what we should be concerned about, and even for how long. Therefore, the primary struggle for our social agenda is between elected officials and the media—not between citizens and our elected leaders.

At the very least, the press has become what I refer to as "the unelected loyal opposition." In days of old, congressional members of the "out" party served as the primary objectors and questioners of the current administration. Today, the press enjoys an aggressive, advocacy role in challenging and questioning those in power. The press claims that it acts on the public's right to know. It has become our political surrogate. In doing so, however, some would argue that the press has contributed to the decline of political parties and citizen participation.

There is a plethora of books about the press that is generating a new vocabulary of media impact: mediacracy, the fourth estate, the electronic commonwealth, and teledemocracy, to name only a few. Few of the books, however, go beyond simple description and general analyses of media impact and influence. I am pleased that *Crime and the American Press* is a welcome exception. It is one of those rare studies that attempts to focus on one specific aspect of media's role in American society.

Crime-related stories comprise the single largest news reporting category of newspapers in America. Why?

By considering whether or not crime stories deserve the amount and prominence of coverage in the media, Lotz tackles many related issues that lie at the very core of the nature and function of the press in America. Should the press simply report the world as it is or attempt to present a more moralistic and uplifting picture? Does the reporting of crime news foster fear and subsequent deterrence, or is its function to generate profits and circulation? Does such news appeal to our legitimate right to know or our morbid sense of curiosity?

In his thoughtful and careful analysis, Lotz reviews the historical (for example, types, rates, amount of coverage), philosophical (for example, information, education, deterrence), theoretical (for example, functional theory, spiral of silence theory, cultivation theory), and pragmatic (for example, advertising, circulation, entertainment) dimensions of crime stories in the press. He finally argues that the press coverage of crime reporting has improved over the years. In fact, in many ways newspapers have become scapegoats for many of society's ills.

Without doubt, this book is an important contribution to political communication and media studies. This study demonstrates both the power and subtleties of media influence in American life. By focusing on a single topic, crime reporting, we gain a full appreciation of the complexity of media influence, ranging from theoretical social implications to specific individual behavior. This approach illuminates the notion of agenda setting and the media. It demonstrates well how the magnitude and frequency of reporting a phenomena create a reality on which we act.

Also of importance is that this study informs us of the news values in America and the biases of columnists in reporting crime and punishment. It challenges common assumptions about such journalistic concepts as objectivity, redlining, news fragmentation, distortion, court coverage, and many more. It investigates journalists' treatment of such issues as drugs, corruption, rights of defendants, death penalty, gun control, and so on. Lotz suggests that in terms of crime reporting, the press tends to be rather conservative in its approach and less sensational than critics have claimed. As a result, this book provides valuable reading for current and future journalists. It will help them gain insight into and appreciation of their potential impact upon society.

Not only is this book a media study but it is also a sociological one, revealing the impact of crime news reporting on our public psyche. Such reporting influences our perceptions of crime and personal safety, which, in turn, influence our feelings of mutual trust, our willingness to help strangers, and even our willingness to attend social groups or volunteer meetings. Lotz demonstrates the impact of crime reporting on our popular culture, exemplified by sensational crime stories and trials made into major motion pictures and television movies. The press and its reporting is very much an active player in the creation of our culture.

If, as McLuhan claimed, the "medium is the message," then we need more study of how media deliver specific messages and to what effect. *Crime and the American Press* is a wonderful example of such a study.

Robert E. Denton, Jr.
Series Editor

Crime
and the
American Press

Chapter One

Justifying Crime News

The power of the press in America is a primordial one. It sets the agenda of public discussion; and this sweeping power is unrestrained. It determines what people will talk about and think about— an authority that in other nations is reserved for tyrants, priests . . . and mandarins.[1]

Most Americans hold firm opinions about the mass media and their effects. They find quite congenial the idea that the media are both powerful and malignant. Power of the press, for example, has attained the status of idiom and draws repeated and uncritical references these days. Commentators making this idea commonplace include Theodore White, the prize-winning campaign biographer. In the quote at the top of this page, he makes the point emphatically.

Nowadays the adjective that first comes to mind is "powerful," but in earlier eras the press was instead considered indispensable. That is, it allowed people to choose and thus was anything but malignant. Classic democratic theory said citizens had to be well informed for democracy to succeed. Once knowledgeable about policies, issues, platforms, and candidates, people could choose wisely among them. A press that:

1. offered a full menu of competing ideas and programs of action and
2. suffered no interference from the government

provided citizens with their best chance of becoming well informed.

When formulating the Bill of Rights, the founding fathers took classic democratic theory to heart, creating the First Amendment to ensure freedom of the press. That the Bill of Rights singles out their line of work for special protection has not escaped journalists' attention. How have they responded to such an honor? This question has given rise to several quite different answers, one by William Henry, who says that journalists show their gratitude for this singular distinction by defending their country, its leaders, and its political system: "Ultimately all journalism is patriotism. If reporters can be said to share a religion, it is devotion to making democracy work. Some believe they serve that end by building respect for leaders, institutions, social order and law enforcement."[2]

ADVERTISING DISORDER

There may be a grain of truth in Henry's argument, but a casual glance at the daily papers reveals less patriotism than gore and less social order than disorder. Crime runs rampant in the American press; papers do such a brisk business in crime that they are, in effect, advertising disorder. In Miami, for instance, not long ago a reporter wrote that some neighborhoods there are under siege in the best of times, with rooftops wrapped in razor wire, while in the worst of times they are engulfed in flames, rioting, and looting.[3]

Newspapers in the rest of the world pursue crime less tenaciously and write about it less extensively, perhaps because those societies experience substantially lower rates of crime and violence. Or perhaps the editors there feel some pressure to keep dark specters out of the headlines on the assumption that this will keep them out of public consciousness as well. Were citizens of other countries to visit the United States, they might be taken aback by the Dickensian horrors depicted in the press.

Just how much space American papers devote to crime and justice has been studied by several researchers over the decades. Political scientist Doris Graber recently did so with Chicago's *Tribune*, *Sun-Times*, and *Daily News*. Examining letters to the editor, editorials, and cartoons, in addition to hard news, she found that the three dailies devoted an average of 25 percent of their items to crime and justice.[4] There is no reason to question her methodology but it could be argued that Chicago or its papers are atypical regarding crime coverage. Therefore, I decided to conduct a more extensive sampling of city papers by examining one from each of four vastly different cities. Unlike Graber, I included only front-page articles of some length. The results of these two studies differ only marginally, as Table 1 shows.

The four newspapers in my sample are mainstream broadsheets, not scandal sheets or supermarket tabloids. Indeed, three of them (the *Chicago Tribune*, *Los Angeles Times*, and *Philadelphia Inquirer*) rank among the country's most respected. Nevertheless, they usher readers into a world

Table 1
News Categories of Four Newspapers' Front Page

News Category	Number	Percent
Crime and Justice	147	30
Domestic Politics and the Economy	81	16
Disasters	81	16
International News	74	15
Miscellaneous Topics	110	22
Total	493	99

of bombings, killings, and the like—hardly what one would expect from papers that claim many Pulitzer Prize recipients on their staff. For them to display such a crime fixation seems odd and improbable.

According to Table 1, 30 percent of the front-page stories in these papers (the fourth of which is the *New Orleans Times-Picayune*) contain tales of police, courts, and criminals. In her study of the three Chicago papers, Graber found 25 percent of the items devoted to these topics. Whether we choose to believe her 25 percent or my 30 percent matters very little, for both suggest the same conclusion: that newspapers in big cities cover crime extensively enough for us to ask "why?"

"FUNCTIONS"

We might try to answer this question by turning to functionalism. This line of thinking originated in biology, where it was readily apparent that the human body "functioned" as a system of interdependent parts, such as the heart and lungs, and that each part performed operations that were necessary for the system to survive and thrive. When sociologists embraced functionalism, they took it in different directions. Several, including most notably Talcott Parsons, concentrated on abstract, sometimes incomprehensible theories while others applied functional analysis to behavior patterns in the real world. Kingsley Davis, for instance, said prostitution was functional; it provided a safety valve for frustrated husbands and thereby helped preserve marriages. Kai

Erikson said that in the colonial period, deviance helped make clear just what the rules and boundaries were between permissible and impermissible behavior in Puritan society.[5]

Functionalism fell into desuetude during the 1970s, but some of its ideas seeped out of academia and into ordinary discourse, particularly when people felt compelled to defend the existence of some practice or social arrangement. People with positions of responsibility in the newspaper industry sometimes feel compelled because critics take them to task for printing an excess of crime and violence. As a rule, the news spokespersons do not accept this criticism. How objectionable can it be for newspapers to report on crime when they have been doing so for more than 300 years? Those who speak for the press presume that any practice that has endured this long must serve some useful purpose.

What that purpose is depends largely on who is asked. The rest of this chapter will look at some of the purported benefits and effects of crime news and suggest that there is little evidence to support them. Chapters 2 and 3 will continue this argument and conclude that crime news does not have significant dysfunctional effects either. In fact, I will go so far as to imply that crime news is not very powerful, a view that flies in the face of widespread claims about the media and their effects.

DETERRENCE AND FEAR

Some newspeople think that crime news benefits society as a whole. They contend that news of police crackdowns, arrests, convictions, and long sentences serve notice to offenders of what may await them. Among the many commentators who have endorsed this thesis, publisher Joseph Pulitzer is the most famous. He said, "There is not a crime . . . there is not a trick, there is not a swindle, there is not a vice which does not live by secrecy. Get things out in the open, describe them, attack them, ridicule them in the press, and . . . public opinion will sweep them away."[6] In Pulitzer's early, hands-on days, when he sat down to compose the front page, filling it with murders and executions, he probably had less magnanimous motives in mind. Pulitzer's gushing enthusiasm aside, most critics would say that he printed crime stories to attract readers among the city's burgeoning working class, many of whom could not understand more complicated news.

Nevertheless, let us assume that he was sincere and believed that crime news does chasten and check would-be criminals. If this hypothesis is valid, then the deterrent effect would presumably cease when newspapers shut down and no crime news reaches print. David Payne tested this thinking by comparing rates of robbery, burglary, and auto theft in four cities before and after strikes there stopped the papers from operating.[7] These three crimes were selected because they are considered rational ones and thus the kind most amenable to deterrence. But Payne found no surge in them after the presses ground to a halt; instead, offenders, apparently oblivious to the strikes, continued plying their trade at the customary pace.

Most criminologists seem unaware that crime news fails to deter, so they have not constructed an explanation of it; it is possible, however, to speculate. To begin with, offenders will not be deterred by news articles unless they have some interest in the news, an ability to read it, and about 40 cents to spend on it. These requirements, though seemingly modest, may prove too demanding, because most offenders do not have a prestigious job or a large disposable income; many do not have an impressive intelligence either. While not all offenders land in jail or prison, most do, particularly if they are career criminals. According to former prison director George Beto, the majority of inmates in prison are not "the intelligent, the cunning, and the glamorous offenders portrayed on television and pictured in the cinema. Rather, they are the poor, the stupid, the inept."[8] This judgment is severe, but it is true that only a modest percentage of inmates are high-school graduates and few have an IQ above 100.[9] Eminent criminologists point out that both IQ score and high-school grades are good predictors of adult criminality.[10] The fact that people deficient in literacy and intelligence commit more crimes and read fewer newspapers offers one explanation for why newspaper reading lacks a deterring effect.

While crime stories may have little impact on would-be offenders, they might substantially influence potential victims, especially those who read the news and take crime items seriously. These stories may discourage readers from wandering into dangerous areas, such as city parks and dark streets. In testing this hypothesis, Linda Heath discovered that reading crime news has no effect on people's fear of crime in their immediate neighborhood; but it does influence their fear of crime elsewhere—some stories heighten it and others dampen it.[11]

Heath argues plausibly that most people want control over what happens to them, so when reading about a crime they may search for hints as to what made the victim vulnerable. If they cannot find any, they will look for traits that distinguish the victim from themselves. Finding such traits, they will be relieved and will conclude, though not very logically, that they will not be the next victim chosen. But if they are unable to determine what made the victim vulnerable or different, they may become more fearful and assume the offender stalks victims at random or, even worse, looks for someone like the reader.

Second, Heath says crimes violate social rules, in some cases many rules and quite flagrantly. If a woman living on a farm in an isolated area goes after her husband while he is asleep and pumps him full of holes with a shotgun, then slices him up and feeds him to the pigs, such an act might please Alfred Hitchcock but it would offend the rest of society. Her actions would violate morés, including marriage vows to love and honor, strictures against cold-blooded killing, and customs regarding proper handling of the dead. These bizarre crimes stick in our memories and keep fear alive in a way that minor offenses do not.

Next, Heath turns to downward comparison theory, which claims that people feel better when contrasting themselves with those who are less fortunate. It is not an endearing quality, but most people like to think that the grass is browner on the other side of the fence. A story of a brutal assault on the East Coast ordinarily will not inspire dread among readers living in Seattle or San Diego. Instead they may experience relief and assume that, unlike citizens living far away, they live in a place of safety. New Yorkers, too, embrace this kind of thinking. While Manhattan, by any objective measure, is crawling with crime, residents hold to the belief that it is safer by several magnitudes than the borough of Brooklyn. This appraisal meets with stiff resistance from citizens of Brooklyn, who say Harlem (in Manhattan) and the South Bronx are far more dangerous. Tell that to someone from the Bronx, however, and you will receive a strident denial.

If functionalists are correct, then crime in the news causes actual crime to decline, because news stories frighten readers into staying in their homes, where the chances of being victimized are relatively small. This is actually two hypotheses: (1) crime news increases fear; and (2) fear reduces the chance of becoming a victim. The second hypothesis will be dealt with later. As for the first one, Heath says that some crime articles raise fears and some lower them. On balance, the two effects cancel each other out. Thus her research implies that crime news does not inspire enough fear overall to reduce the crime rate.

INFORMATION

Few Americans would ever consider holding newspapers responsible for criminality, so when hundreds of thousands of predators commit unscrupulous acts each year, it is not newspaper reporters who receive the blame for them. If they were blamed, they would quickly deny the charge and say that they rail against crime. Maybe they do, but according to the functionalist view, this may not be enough. Perhaps newspapers should also provide surveillance.

Consider what it means to a society for its members to have a constant stream of public information about events in the world. One positive consequence (function) of such surveillance is that it provides warnings about imminent threats of danger. Forewarned, the population can mobilize and protect itself.[12]

Thus weather reports and predictions enable readers and listeners to take precautions such as bundling up or applying sun block. Weather is just one of many practical, mundane issues about which people want their newspaper to provide helpful information. Papers could offer the latest data on crime—for instance, which street corners and subway stations pose the greatest threat to pedestrians. But instead of supplying such useful information, crime reports normally detail one crime at a time and steer away from generalizations. "If they sound like copies from the police blotter, the explanation is that this is what they are."[13] As a rule, they do not try to reach general conclusions about the nature of criminality; nor when dwelling on facts and details do they specify the practical import of these facts. Readers, with no theory of criminality to go by, cannot see what point is being made, what larger picture the facts of the case fit. So if they want to know how best to protect their tape deck or their daughter, the paper will not help. Except for rare occasions, newspaper crime stories lack this kind of "surveillance."

SIGNIFICANCE

How important are crime stories—enough to bump other news off the front page and into the paper's midsection? Herbert Gans says that a story is suitable for publication if it is important or interesting. And one of the key elements of importance is how many people the issue or event affects. "The most important story of all is one that affects every American."[14] Other researchers say that impact or importance is the primary criterion newspaper editors use to select and place stories. But consider the issue of the *Philadelphia Inquirer* from August 9, 1985. That day readers encountered the following stories only if they read as far as page 7:

1. Spokesmen for India revealed that it had developed the ability to produce plutonium, a vital component in the manufacture of nuclear power and nuclear weapons.
2. President Marcos accepted an award from the Soviet Union and took the opportunity to chide the United States for interfering in Philippine affairs.

The development of plutonium in India seemed ominous. While nuclear weaponry in the hands of the superpowers constitutes an ever-present danger, in third-world countries, where instability and fanaticism are not uncommon, the threat may be greater. It might also raise questions about priorities, given India's monumental problems of poverty, overpopulation, unemployment, and cultural factionalism.

At the time of the Marcos article, he enjoyed considerable power and close friendship with the Reagans. Hence, relations between the two governments should have been cordial, but this story hinted otherwise.

Someone reading this article back in August 1985 would not have fore-
seen Marcos's fall from power or the U.S. role in that fall, but this story
served as a red flag and put readers on the alert that something eventually might happen to him. Thus, it might be argued that such a story
was too important to be pushed back to the paper's midsection.

Having assigned these stories to page 7, the editors put a story about
the killing of a go-go dancer in a Camden bar on page 1. The question
is why, what made this so important? As defined by journalists, importance usually means how many people are affected, how seriously
and how immediately. This story affected the victim, offender, their
relatives, and the other bar patrons. It seems that stories affecting so
few could be covered in two or three paragraphs and stuck back among
the ads for bunions and hemorrhoids treatment.

To be sure, some crimes merit front-page attention, for instance, mass
murders, political assassinations, Wall Street scandals, and the like. Others deserve press consideration because they have significant ramifications; the Tawana Brawley case in New York fits this category. Miss
Brawley, at age 15, disappeared from her home in November 1987 and
turned up four days later in nearby Wappingers Falls inside a plastic
garbage bag. Her advisers and family said she had been kidnapped,
beaten, raped, tortured, and sodomized in the woods by six white men,
who had chopped off part of her hair, smeared feces over her, written
"nigger" and other words in charcoal on her chest, then stuffed her in
the bag and left her to die in the cold winter night.

Later, another version of the events began to emerge. Witnesses said
they saw Miss Brawley climb into the bag after she spent several days
in the Wappingers Fall apartment where her family used to live. Medical
personnel and FBI experts found no sign of malnutrition, exposure,
trauma, rape, or sodomy. Her nose and ears had been stuffed with
cotton, suggesting that she was being protected against infection. The
charcoal-like substance turned out to be cotton clothing that had been
burned and dipped in water, and such material was found in the apartment. No traces were found on her to suggest she had spent time in
the woods. A grant jury and the *New York Times* concluded that the
earlier version was concocted in its entirety.

This story had important implications for crime, law enforcement, and
race relations. It followed on the heels of other highly publicized cases
of blacks being victimized; in New York City, hardly a soul alive did not
know of the incidents involving Eleanor Bumpurs, Michael Stewart, and
Michael Griffith (the latter of which was known as the Howard Beach
case). If the public accepted the original version of what happened to
Tawana Brawley, the reputations of Dutchess County police would have
been damaged beyond repair; the governor and state attorney general
were also under a cloud of suspicion as racists. But if this version proved

wrong, the public might regard future claims of racist crimes and police cover-ups with a more skeptical eye. Thus, the Brawley case was fraught with implications and eminently deserving of press attention. The great majority of cases, however, bear little resemblance to this and cannot be considered nearly as significant.

MIRROR ON THE WORLD

Years ago as a graduate student at the University of Washington, I taught a course in deviant behavior. For reasons that now escape me, I informed my mother back in Illinois that I was lecturing on crime, delinquency, prostitution, mental illness, drugs, and suicide. Having lived in an era before psychology displaced moral philosophy, she found my choice of topics repellent and in a return letter asked why I did not present the other side, which, I presume, meant conforming and "virtuous" behaviors. It may be that journalists face this same pressure, to emphasize good news instead of bad. Journalists respond by saying that they write about the world as it is, warts and all, not some idealized Norman Rockwell version.

This snappy retort silences questioners, but how accurate is it—do reporters hold a mirror up to society and reflect life faithfully? In the past, journalists tended to say yes. They not only used the mirror as a convenient metaphor but sometimes made it part of the paper's title, as in the *London Mirror* and the *Los Angeles Mirror*. But journalists are not omniscient; they cannot see all that happens, nor could they report it if they did. Newspapers receive about ten times as much information as they can process. In most cases, reporters assigned to a beat rely on a small number of sources, each of which has particular biases and blind spots.

How unmirrorlike papers can be shows in their crime coverage. Most newspapers in America stress murders, although by all accounts this is among the rarest crimes in actual occurrence. Practically every study of crime news reports the same finding: that crimes of violence receive more attention than other types of crimes. Property crimes, for instance, probably outnumber violent ones by more than ten to one but receive comparatively little attention.

Journalists focus on novelty, as memorialized forever in the phrase "man bites dog." When that happens, a story is bound to result. Reporters claim that it is not their job to write about the typical events of everyday life. So they do not mention the thousands of safe landings at airports, only the crashes. News means new, out of the ordinary. This entails crime without perspective; no reporter would say, "Yesterday, 46,000 students in Houston's junior high schools behaved as perfect ladies and gentlemen, except for Billy Bob Puckett, who blew his principal away with his trusty Winchester." Choosing events for their novelty virtually ensures that newspapers will not accurately reflect what is happening most of the time in society. Most students of the news media take this to be so obvious that they do not bother to mention it.

CIRCULATION

Fear, deterrence, and significance are justifications for printing crime news that make it appear laudable. But other observers say that the real motive behind this practice is to boost circulation and profits. They buttress this argument with a little history. In 1833 Benjamin Day founded the *New York Sun* and in so doing inadvertently started a revolution. Hiring George Wisner to write several daily columns on the police courts proved to be a master stroke, for Wisner brought the court and its parade of characters to life for the city's readers: "Bridget McNunn got drunk and threw a pitcher at Mr. Ellis. . . . Bridget said she was the mother of 3 little orphans—God bless their dear souls—and if she went to prison they would choke to death for want of something to eat. Committed."[15] The *Sun*'s circulation rose rapidly, thanks in large part to Wisner's court reporting, the first of its kind in America.

Soon afterward, James Gordon Bennett founded the *New York Herald*. Bennett, who had far more writing talent than Day, also had a gift for offending New York's establishment, members of which retaliated by giving him a horsewhipping. He carried on crusades to rid the newspapers of euphemisms and in the process became the first American editor to use terms such as arms, legs, and pants. To modern readers it seems scarcely credible, but some women at that time were said to faint at the sight of such words in print, and soon moral war was declared against the editor and his paper. Though beset by both arson and beatings, the paper and the man continued, emphasizing sex, crime, and upper-class misconduct. Circulation soared.

Some say Bennett also introduced the interview and sensationalism. When prostitute Helen Jewett died of hatchet wounds in a brothel, suspicion fell on her last customer. Six-penny papers covered the murder in the dry, abbreviated fashion then standard, but Mr. Bennett, ever the innovator, broke with Victorian conventions of taste and visited the brothel, where he carefully inspected the body and generally played the role of Columbo. "He saw the woman who had discovered the body, asked her everything a curious busybody could think of, and recounted the conversation in dialogue form to his readers—the first interview. He reconstructed the life of the girl in that 'wicked house.' "[16] Not long after this, the *Herald*'s circulation tripled, and eventually it equalled that of the *London Times*.

About 50 years later, Joseph Pulitzer purchased the *New York World*, a dreary rag and consistent money loser that had possibilities that only he foresaw. He instituted changes immediately, giving foreign and political news less emphasis and crime and tragedy more. To tailor the paper to the modest reading skills of the city's working class, he introduced large, provocative headlines, for example, BAPTIZED IN BLOOD and LET ME DIE! LET ME DIE! Evidently these innovations succeeded, because within three years circulation of the previously moribund *World* jumped from 15,000 to 250,000.

William Randolph Hearst found Pulitzer's achievement so impressive that he decided to enter the world of New York journalism himself. In 1895 he took control of the *New York Journal* and ushered in a "shrieking, gaudy, sensation-loving, devil-may-care kind of journalism."[17] Using scare headlines, large type, cartoons, and editorials, he pressured McKinley relentlessly until he got what he wanted—the Spanish–American War. Once war was under way, Hearst sought to make Teddy Roosevelt into a hero. In this he proved successful. Years later he would work even harder to destroy Franklin Roosevelt.

Hearst made murder, scandal, adultery, and disaster his prime topics of discourse; he violated the cardinal rule of journalism by urging reporters to use their imaginations and instructed headline writers to emphasize the story's most shocking detail, no matter how trivial a role that detail played in the story. During that time, New York City had a much smaller population, greater competition among papers, and a lower level of literacy than today. Despite such obstacles, one day in 1900 the *Journal* sold 1,500,000 copies, a startling accomplishment.

The well-known formula remained intact from Day to Hearst: write breathless prose about crime, violence, and disaster, and readers will beat a path to your door. Although this formula worked well for more than a century, its effectiveness is vanishing today. According to Ben Bagdikian, people relying on this formula have seen their papers swimming in red ink since World War II, while circulation giants such as the *Wall Street Journal*, *USA Today*, and *New York Times* have won readers without reporting much on street crime. Papers that banked on such crime to stay afloat have been going under. Bagdikian gives several reasons for this:

1. Long ago, people bought papers at newsstands or from noisy street hawkers strategically placed. Screaming headlines augmented sales, including those about sordid crimes. Today, vendors are disappearing, so headlines cannot work their former magic.

2. Advertising now accounts for four-fifths of newspaper profits, circulation one-fifth. Advertisers normally prefer to buy space in the city's best-selling paper, unless it caters to the very poor, the very old, or the very young. Papers know that the way to appeal to advertisers is by selling subscriptions to large numbers of comfortable suburbanites.

3. The major drawback of newspapers that dwell on crime and violence is that these topics appeal much more to the poor, black, and less educated segments of the population than to the well-to-do and educated.[18]

While Bagdikian is probably correct in this analysis, the overwhelming majority of people in America seem to believe that crime news sells. Even those who are very familiar with the field seem to think so. It has been suggested that concentrating on crime and violence allowed Rupert Murdoch's *New York Post* to experience an unparalleled rise in circulation. To be sure, the *Post* did carry crime news, but other analysts concluded that the rise in circulation had more to do with the paper's bingo contests. In any case, the fast-growing paper soon became the fastest shrinking paper when the bingo games stopped, even though the crime stories remained. As for Murdoch, he lost $150 million over ten years, and his successor is losing just as badly.

Stories about crime help to sell papers, but so do sports, puzzles, horoscopes, stock tables, weather, political columnists, comics, food sections, and just about everything else. The problem is that crime alone does not keep a paper going. "Newspapers, operating within a restricted geographical area, cannot survive . . . by limiting their appeal to a narrow segment"—which, in effect, is what crime-heavy papers have done.[19]

ENTERTAINMENT

Herbert Gans says that to be suitable or newsworthy an item must be important or interesting. There are many commentators who believe that crime news is interesting. Kai Erikson has asserted that newspapers provide readers the kind of entertainment they once got by observing public hangings or people being put in stocks and pillories.[20] Just why readers find crime so interesting is unclear: do they identify with the victims or the offenders, or is their interest in crime due to its being shocking and unpredictable? Or perhaps crime news is not really so exciting after all. If the murder story of the go-go dancer in Camden is typical (it went into boring detail about names, addresses, and style of clothing worn), then much crime news is tedious and plodding.

Measuring how interesting crime articles are requires comparing them with other news items, so I did this with stories in the *Chicago Tribune*, *Los Angeles Times*, *New Orleans Times-Picayune*, and *Philadelphia Inquirer* during late July and early August in 1985. The following list includes my nomination of the 25 most interesting stories of that period. The list shows that crime *can* be interesting but usually is not.

1. Weather	Philadelphia Inquirer	Hikers' Luck Ended When the Mountain Gods Roared
2. Killing	Chicago Tribune	The Day a Broken Man Cried
3. Poverty	Los Angeles Times	True Victims of Poverty: The Children
4. Killing	Chicago Tribune	Police Track a Murderer in Shadowy "Other" Chicago
5. Killing	Los Angeles Times	Rage Over Apartheid, But Was Victim a Traitor?
6. Drinking	Philadelphia Inquirer	Thirsty Trade: Soviet Soldiers Tank Up on Vodka
7. Child Abuse	Chicago Tribune	Satanism Haunts Tales of Child Sex Abuse
8. Killing	Philadelphia Inquirer	Fury, Stones--And a Body Ablaze
9. Poverty	Los Angeles Times	Poor Share Work Ethic, U.S. Dream
10. Violence	Chicago Tribune	Cabrini Kids Helped Out of the Shadows
11. War	Chicago Tribune	POW Experimenters Reportedly Set Free
12. Religion	Los Angeles Times	Agency Apologizes for Christian Letter

13. Illness	Times-Picayune	Chaplain Offers Sustenance by Lending a Sympathetic Ear
14. Travel	Times-Picayune	Stowaways Elude Cruise Ship Cops Until Last Day
15. Bombing	Philadelphia Inquirer	Nixon: Weighed Using the Bomb
16. Weather	Chicago Tribune	Icy Bay, Arctic Winds Can't Stop Soviet Woman from Defecting
17. Poverty	Los Angeles Times	Case History of a 20-Year War on Poverty
18. Rebellion	Los Angeles Times	Foreigners Flee Uganda, Tell of Shooting, Looting
19. Marriage	Times-Picayune	Divorce Granted to Child Bride
20. Courts	Philadelphia Inquirer	60 Years Ago, Evolution Was on Trial Here
21. Youth	Los Angeles Times	The Pepsi Generation--Gray Area
22. Gambling	Chicago Tribune	Gentle Giant Bullied Into Paying $50,000
23. Courts	Los Angeles Times	Girl Deformed in Acid Attack Testifies at Trial
24. Sport	Times-Picayune	Trophy Tarpon Crashes Trip, Gives Anglers Shot at Record
25. Religion	Los Angeles Times	Pope Beatifies Nun Who Died to Save Virginity, Forgives Killer

Crime is prominent in five of the top eight stories, but after that it appears sparingly. Straight crime articles arouse only a modest amount of interest; something special is needed. *Chicago Tribune* writers sometimes supply this by emphasizing the point of view of either the victim or offender or by dwelling on the eerie atmosphere. Also, crime in other cultures can be made interesting, as was the case in stories about South Africa. Aside from the African locale and the *Tribune* writing, though, crime stories were not usually entrancing.

According to Leo Bogart, news, to be interesting, must arouse readers' emotions, which can be accomplished by writing about events that are inherently dramatic or by creating excitement through style and imagery.[21] But reporters assigned to write about crime are generally less educated and less competent than their peers. They earn little pay and less esteem. Some papers take pride in not having police reporters at all—so symbolic are they of hack writing.

Bogart has done extensive research on what kinds of items newspaper readers find most appealing. He found considerably more interest in crime than in puzzles, horoscopes, sports, Hollywood entertainers, and cultural events and reviews. But he also found more interest in energy problems, accidents and disasters, weather, travel, and letters to the editor than in crime. Furthermore, when newspapers in New York were on strike, he asked residents what they missed most. Crime was not mentioned frequently. Indeed, it was hardly mentioned at all.[22]

CONCLUSION

For hundreds of years, political philosophers have said that the public must have access to information if democracy is to survive. Thinking such as this led to the First Amendment protection of the free press. All of us may agree that the free press is a desirable thing to have, but what does the modern press do with its freedom? What does it print more of than anything else? Crime. Not patriotism or civic boosterism, not democracy or capitalism or domestic politics. Most newspapers in America's large cities appear to be bent on creating the disquieting impression that crime and disorder are rampant. To what end?

Those who speak on behalf of newspapers say that crime news serves positive functions either for the newspaper or for society. And they are not alone in this view. Mass communication specialist Mitchell Stephens agrees.

Societies depend on news of violations of the law to reinforce understanding of their laws and fear of their punishments; they depend on accounts of the out of the ordinary to strengthen the consensus on what qualifies as ordinary. . . . [E]ach shared reaction—fear, grief, outrage—reawakens a sense of shared destiny and shared purpose.[23]

The common view is that crime news interests readers, who therefore buy the paper, read about some felony, and thereby increase the paper's circulation and profits. Once upon a time, say, in the era of Hearst, Pulitzer, and yellow journalism, that may have been valid.

That, however, was nearly a century ago. In the ensuing years, American society has changed in ways that have undermined this line of thinking. First of all, citizens can now turn to other fare, much of it more exciting and evocative than news items (we can read of crime in novels and thrillers, watch it on television or at the movies; in addition, there are many sources of entertainment today that do not revolve around crime). People have a range of stimulating experiences from which to choose and more money to buy them. Second, newspapers rarely break the news these days. They generally have only one edition, which takes many hours to prepare and distribute, in contrast to radio and television, which can bring listeners the latest developments. This renders newspapers old and thus less stimulating.

Third, newspaper readers nowadays tend to be more educated, influential, and well-to-do adults, that is, people whose taste does not usually run to crime and violence. Some Americans like to find out about mad slashers, and some have a special fondness for splatter movies, but these are not, as a rule, the people who read daily papers religiously. Fourth, editors favor stories about conflict, probably thinking that readers will feel the same way. But when they assign the least able reporters to cover crime and expect them to use the same dry, formulaic prose style traditionally taught in journalism classes, the result is dull and pedestrian.

These and other developments (cited by Bagdikian) have conspired to undercut the impact of newspaper crime articles. Their functions (if there were any) were never automatic but contingent. As American society underwent rapid social change over the years, conditions that may have made crime news functional at one time tended to disappear. Readers changed markedly in income, education, sophistication, and style of life. One hundred years ago, for instance, there were no public high schools in the city of New York. Social and technological changes took place too. It is a different world than when Pulitzer and Hearst were fighting one another, and McKinley was sitting in the White House. Expecting crime news to maintain its same functions through all of these changes is probably unrealistic.

NOTES

1. Theodore White, *The Making of the President, 1972* (New York: Bantam, 1973), p. 327.

2. William Henry III, "News as Entertainment," in *What's News,* ed. Elie Abel (San Francisco: Institute for Contemporary Studies, 1981), p. 153.

3. Liz Doup, "Miami on Edge," *Charlotte Observer*, November 23, 1988, p. 38A.

4. Doris Graber, *Crime News and the Public* (New York: Praeger, 1980), p. 26.

5. Talcott Parsons, *The Social System* (Glencoe, IL: Free Press, 1951); Kingsley Davis, "The Sociology of Prostitution," *American Sociological Review* 2 (October 1937): 746–755; Kai Erikson, *Wayward Puritans* (New York: Wiley, 1966).

6. W. A. Swanberg, *Pulitzer* (New York: Scribner's, 1967), p. 462.

7. David Payne, "Newspapers and Crime," *Journalism Quarterly* 51 (Winter 1974): 607–612.

8. Bruce Jackson, *Law and Disorder* (Urbana: University of Illinois Press, 1984), p. 218.

9. *Report to the Nation on Crime and Justice* (Washington, D.C.: Department of Justice, 1988), p. 48; W. J. Estelle, Jr., *Fact Sheet* (Huntsville: Texas Department of Corrections, 1982).

10. Travis Hirschi and Michael Hindelang, "Intelligence and Delinquency," *American Sociological Review* 47 (August 1977): 571–587; Kenneth Polk, "Delinquency and Adult Criminal Careers," in *Criminal Behavior*, ed. Delos Kelly (New York: St. Martin's, 1980), pp. 148–149.

11. Linda Heath, "Impact of Newspaper Crime Reports on Fear of Crime," *Journal of Personality and Social Psychology* 47 (August 1984): 263–276.

12. Charles Wright, *Mass Communication* (New York: Random House, 1986), p. 14.

13. Graber, *Crime News and the Public*, p. 47.

14. Herbert Gans, *Deciding What's News* (New York: Vintage, 1980), p. 151.

15. Frank Mott, *American Journalism* (New York: Macmillan, 1962), p. 223.

16. Helen MacGill Hughes, *News and the Human Interest Story* (New York: Greenwood Press, 1968), p. 12.

17. Edwin Emery and Michael Emery, *The Press and America* (Englewood Cliffs, NJ: Prentice-Hall, 1984), p. 282.

18. Ben Bagdikian, *The Effete Conspiracy* (New York: Harper and Row, 1972), p. 7.

19. Leo Bogart, *The Press and the Public* (Hillsdale, NJ: Erlbaum, 1989), p. 254; Mitchell Stephens, "Crime Doesn't Pay: Except on the Newsstands," *Washington Journalism Review* 3 (December 1981): 39.

20. Kai Erikson, "Notes on the Sociology of Deviance," in *The Other Side*, ed. Howard Becker (New York: Free Press, 1964), p. 14.

21. Bogart, *The Press and the Public*, p. 270.

22. Ibid., p. 301.

23. Mitchell Stephens, *A History of News* (New York: Viking, 1988), p. 35.

Crime over Time

John Maynard Keynes once said that "practical men who believe themselves to be quite exempt from any intellectual influences are usually slaves to some defunct economist."[1] According to this view, most people cling to ideas that were diffused long ago and have since been dismissed as invalid by modern specialists and theoreticians. In a sense, Keynes may have understated the case, for what he says about economics could probably be said about other fields as well, including history and criminology. Common ideas about crime in the past may be those of some defunct historian. In this chapter, two such ideas will be confronted: one a variant of functionalism, and the other, temperocentrism.

SOCIETAL SURVEILLANCE

Chapter 1 considered surveillance at the individual level, but it is also possible to have surveillance at the societal level: when crime rates rise, newspapers react by printing more crime stories, which in turn helps galvanize police, judges, and legislators into action. Conversely, with low crime rates, crime stories will be few, because no pressing need exists for officials to be alerted. Therefore, high crime rates should be accompanied by ample crime news, and low rates by little news. Functionalists might thus predict high rates and extensive news currently in the United States but low crime rates and little news in the United States in the past and in other countries today.

IS CRIME COMMON NOW?

For years the FBI was the basic source of crime data, as it compiled reports sent in from police departments around the nation; these Uniform Crime Reports (UCR) gave particular attention to the Crime Index offenses, that is, murder, rape, robbery, aggravated assault, burglary, larceny/theft, and motor vehicle theft. Criminologists can turn either to the number of offenses police record or to the number of arrests they make, but since police fail to make an arrest in most cases, arrests are not an adequate measure of crime in America.

Some crimes go unreported because there are no witnesses, while others are witnessed but not reported because people assume that doing so would be a waste of time as police would not catch the offender or return the stolen property. Even when crimes are witnessed and reported, police may not record them, because they want to avoid the paperwork or because they do not regard the matter as a criminal violation. Therefore, even the number of offenses recorded may understate the actual extent of crime.

During the 1980s, FBI data consistently showed per year about 20,000 murders, 85,000 rapes, 500,000 robberies, 700,000 aggravated assaults, 1,000,000 motor vehicle thefts, 3,000,000 burglaries, and 7,000,000 larcenies. This means 12,000,000 index crimes per year in a population of about 240,000,000 or one such crime a year during the 1980s for every 20 persons. Criminologists cite these data but treat them skeptically, especially when they are used to make statements about changes over time. A small change in reporting or recording could affect estimates of change dramatically.[2]

Given the deficiencies of the Uniform Crime Reports, some criminologists have turned to victimization surveys, in which thousands of households each year are interviewed and asked how many and what kind of victimizations were incurred. By and large, victim surveys are more credible than UCR data, although we cannot assume that they are perfect either. They suffer from two principal defects, namely, memory decay and ignorance. Memory decay means that the respondent being interviewed forgets one or more incidents that he or some other member of the household experienced during the past six months or year. Ignorance means that someone in the household was victimized but the victim never told the respondent, so the respondent could not relate it to the interviewer.

Both memory decay and ignorance lead victim surveys to undercount the actual number of crimes. Even so, in 1988, according to the National Crime Survey, 23,000,000 households were touched by crime, some of them several times. This was one-fourth of all households, and among urban households and households in the western states, the figure that year was even higher, over 30 percent.[3] Judging by the victimization data, then, crime in today's America is widespread. While not all crimes are traumatic for the victims (some of whom, remember, do not recall the offense a few months later when asked in surveys), clearly the crime problem is extensive. Thus the first part of the functionalist surveillance argument seems correct, for crime in society and crime in the news are both currently abundant.

CRIME IN OTHER SOCIETIES

The functionalist argument has other implications, too, for instance, that other societies have less crime news (let us assume this is so) and lower crime rates. Few criminologists have diligently mined the data on cross-cultural crime rates. It seems that not very many nations maintain accurate statistics on crime, and some of those that do, have not shared such statistics with visiting scholars. But Sir Leon Radzinowicz has published figures comparing crime data from America and Europe and has concluded that our crime problem looks much more serious than theirs.

"There are as many murders in Manhattan each year as in the whole of England and Wales. . . . Detroit, with much the same population as Northern Ireland, has even in these grim days five times the murders."[4] He added that New York has 31 times the robberies of London, and Philadelphia has 44 times the homicides of Vienna, despite similar population sizes. Los Angeles, he said, has more drug addiction than all of western Europe.

Outside Europe and England, Japan is one of the few countries generally thought to have good statistics on crime. Indeed, Japanese law enforcement agencies count crimes so much more accurately than American agencies that statistical comparisons between the two countries are suspect. Even so, Japan's crime rate is low. For every 279 robberies New York experienced in 1979, Tokyo had one. With 8,500,000 people, Tokyo suffered only one instance of a burglar invading a home and killing someone.[5]

Any time of the day or night, apparently, a man or woman can walk through a Tokyo alley or sit in one of its parks without incident.

No muggings.
No pickpockets.
No violence.
No thieves.
This is a condition you feel as soon as you arrive, and if you are used to, say, New York, the feeling you have in Tokyo of safety and security—walking down the street with $500 in an unbuttoned pocket—is so liberating as to be almost heady.[6]

Testimonials by visitors to Japan might be questioned, and the Rad-zinowicz data might be dismissed as old. More recent data do exist; the Justice Department's Bureau of Crime Statistics not long ago compared crime rates in the United States with those in Europe and in Australia–Canada–New Zealand (the three countries treated as one entity). The report noted that from 1980 to 1984, the homicide rate in the U.S. varied from 7.9 to 10.5 per 100,000 people, while in Europe the rate was less than 2, and in Australia–Canada—New Zealand it was less than 3.

Rapes also proved more common in America than elsewhere, as our rate was 36 per 100,000. In western Europe, the rate was a modest 4.8, and in Australia–Canada–New Zealand, the rate of rapes ranged from a low of 10.5 to 14.1 during the period examined. Theft and auto theft rates were lowest in western Europe, where they were only about half as high as the rates in the United States and in Australia–Canada–New Zealand.[7] Cross-cultural statistical comparisons are always hazardous, because of differences in definitions and agencies doing the counting, but most comparisons lead to the conclusion that the United States has more violence than most other countries. Thus, on this question, there is some support for the functionalist surveillance argument.

U.S. CRIME IN THE PAST

The functionalist argument also implies that America experienced less crime in the past than it experiences nowadays. Very few criminologists have invested their careers in tracing variations in the rate of crime over the past century. There are some historians, however, who have studied a related question: the changing extent of violence in America. In part, their efforts were a response to interest in this topic generated by the killings of John Kennedy, Martin Luther King, and Robert Kennedy. These historians found that violence has been present throughout society over the past two centuries.

Richard Maxwell Brown has called attention to the existence of two types of violence: negative and positive. While the former usually has been condemned by the society, the latter has been condoned, because the goals seemed worthwhile and the means unavoidable and thus excusable.

American life has been characterized by continuous and often intense vio-lence. It is not merely that violence has accompanied such negative aspects of our history as criminal activity, political assassination, and racial conflict. On the contrary, violence has formed a seamless web with some of the most positive events of U.S. history: independence (revolutionary violence), the freeing of the slaves and the preservation of the Union (Civil War violence), the occupation of the land (Indian wars), the stabilization of frontier society (vigilante violence) . . . [8]

Yet not all violence is defined as crime; nor are all crimes violent—examples include theft and victimless crimes.

No one denies that thorny measurement problems complicate attempts to compare crime rates from different cultures; the comparison of crime rates in the same country at different periods can be just as daunting. To make these comparisons valid requires that similar crimes measured at different times be equally visible to witnesses, equally likely to be reported by them, and equally likely to be recorded by police (and such records kept and made accessible to future historians and criminologists). Few such requirements have been met.

Recordkeeping in the distant past was often haphazard. Many cities did not have a police department 150 years ago. Before modern police departments came into being, the prevailing system employed watchmen. Murders now are widely regarded as the one offense best counted by the criminal justice apparatus, but many of them were not even reported to police in the nineteenth century. To some extent this was because police were not then thought of as strictly a crime control agency. Philadelphia police in 1898 had only 15 detectives, and not one of them was assigned to investigate homicides.[9]

Despite the methodological morass, historians of crime seem to agree on the direction crime rates have taken over the past 150 years. First, they contend that rates have risen sharply since about 1960. In the United States, as elsewhere, they rely on official data for these estimates, and the official data here show substantial increases, though it could be that the increases reflect a greater willingness to report crime, especially rapes. The UCR are often cited as the only evidence of crime's rise. Table 2 shows the percentage increases estimated by the FBI between 1960 and 1980.[10]

Second, they tend to agree that during the latter two-thirds of the nineteenth century the crime rates dropped. Naturally, the evidence for such a drop is not completely consistent, for some crimes followed a different pattern than others. But data from arrests, convictions, and coroner reports in the case of murders have been pieced together by historians to give the impression of declining incidence of crime.

Third, most historians who have examined crime data for the period from 1900 to about 1960 agree that the rates were relatively low, particularly at the beginning. When these figures are compared with estimated rates of crime before 1900 and after 1960, the resulting distribution is a U-shaped curve, with crime rates very high before 1850 and very high after 1960 but sloping strongly downward as the middle of the period is approached, say, around 1900.

This means that if we focus on the period of 1900 to 1980 or 1990, the first half of the proposed U-shaped curve drops out of the picture, leaving only the right half, which shows a steeply rising slope. *During*

Table 2
Rate Changes for Index Crimes

	1960–1970	1970–1980
Murder	56%	31%
Forcible Rape	95%	99%
Robbery	186%	42%
Aggravated Assault	92%	79%
Burglary	113%	56%
Larceny–Theft	233%	268%
Motor Vehicle Theft	150%	9%

the most recent 80 or 90 years, historians believe, the United States and other western nations have undergone a dramatic increase in crime. If we focus on this limited period alone (and not the longer one), then the crime rates provide some support for the functionalist surveillance view that crime used to be less common than it is nowadays.

CRIME NEWS IN THE PAST

The functionalist surveillance argument implies that when crime rates were low (around the turn of the century) stories of crime made up a small proportion of front-page news articles. With little crime happening, newspapers should not be sounding the warning on crime. They could give the front page over to other matters that were more pressing at the time.

To see what newspapers had to say about crime and how much attention they gave it, I examined three newspapers (the *Boston Globe, Chicago Tribune,* and *San Francisco Chronicle*) for the first two Monday-through-Friday weeks in April for the years 1895, 1900, 1905, 1910, and 1915 (see Table 3). Stories were included if they began on page 1 and continued for at least ten paragraphs. Next, they were classified by topic to see how common crime and justice articles were in relation to other topics. Crime and justice proved to be a popular source of news articles

Table 3
Number of Front-Page Stories by Topic

Category	Frequency
Crime and Justice	187
The International Scene	165
Politics	132
Religion	36
Business	22
Accidents	17
Deaths and Obituaries	17
Other	101
Total	677

in the early part of this century. Among the 677 front-page articles at least ten paragraphs long, 28 percent dealt with this topic. This figure is nearly as high as the 30 percent I found when examining present-day newspapers (in Chapter 1) and casts grave doubt on the functionalist surveillance argument. Apparently, news readers were inundated with crime articles many years ago though crime was not such a serious problem.

Contrary to the functionalist surveillance approach, crime news may abound when crime rates are low. In an era when crime is rather uncommon, one offense may stand out vividly, in effect, crying for attention. Roger Lane points out that in the 1890s, armed robbery must have been a rarity, for a holdup in the Bronx received coverage in Philadelphia—on the front page.[11] Apparently, despite low crime rates, newspapers write about crime just as much as in other times.

TEMPEROCENTRISM

While the societal surveillance argument deals with the *amount* of crime news in times past, temperocentrism dwells on its *nature*. Temperocentrists view the past as a quaint time when things were better, unlike today, when the world is uniquely contentious.[12] They find today's journalists to be rude, cynical, and unpatriotic, to have crippled the Johnson and Nixon administrations and driven both men from the Oval Office.

On the other hand, they regard journalists of the distant past fondly, describing them as genteel men who wore fedoras, carried walking sticks and calling cards. These men, it is claimed, never stooped to anything unseemly. They did not even rush from office to office or use the telephone. That, at least, is the conclusion of David Halberstam.[13] Modern presidents yearn for those halcyon days when the press was docile, not digging up dirt, crime, and corruption. Ordinarily, the temperocentrist position is asserted as fact, not tested by turning to relevant data. First, let us examine the argument by looking at how crime articles were written in the distant past. Afterward, we will turn to political coverage (mostly of presidents) of the past.

Temperocentrists do not focus on the amount of news but its tone, which they find excessively aggressive and muckraking. They contend that in earlier eras it was much milder. If we apply this line of thinking to crime news, it suggests that offenders may even have been lionized by newspaper articles many decades ago. I sampled crime articles from the *Boston Globe*, *Chicago Tribune*, and *San Francisco Chronicle* in early April for the years 1895, 1900, 1905, 1910, and 1915. They did not ordinarily depict offenders as heroes (as they had Jesse James earlier), but they did sometimes celebrate what virtues they found in these men. When Oliver Perry escaped from an asylum in New York, several papers spoke flatteringly of his skills and expressed amazement at his ingenious escape.

One newspaper carried a story celebrating the intellectual gifts of a brilliant poet imprisoned in Stillwater, Minnesota, but with few inmates like him, most praise dwelt less on offenders' cerebral assets than their physical assets.

Sam, tall and of powerful physique, lies on a board in the morgue, with his massive jaws apart and his long black hair tumbled to one side. . . . The dead bandit was a powerful man in life. Dr. David Powell, who performed the autopsy, says he never saw a better specimen of physical manhood.[14]

Apparently, offenders were regarded as less threatening in that period. Reporters were not compelled by journalistic convention to write about them in uniformly derogatory terms.

Virtues were not the only traits of offenders brought to readers' attention. Race and ethnicity were also duly noted. It has been said that when papers around the turn of the century mentioned Italians, it was usually in the context of crime. The three papers I sampled mentioned Italians as such in several crime stories—and not very flatteringly. One article in the *Boston Globe* described a violent argument that began when an Italian "became enraged," as something happened that caused his "Neapolitan blood to boil." Other stories in the news pointedly reminded readers that the Mafia and the Black Hand were around and heavily involved in crime and violence.

Newspapers of the turn of the century mentioned black offenders, too, but not in a way that emphasized their threat potential. Instead stories tended to make them the butt of humor, as in this article taken from the *Chicago Tribune* of 1915:

Robert Jones and Robert Graham, colored boys . . . were on trial in Judge Dever's court yesterday. Russell Bickford, a farmer, told the court he had an old horse which he had tried to sell for $5, but, finding no buyers, he had made a dicker with the Jones boy to swap the steed for eighteen chickens. . . .

Thirteen plump fowls . . . were duly delivered . . . with Jones' promise that he sho' would come across with the rest in a day or two. The next morning Mrs. Mary Christy . . . went out to the henhouse and found it empty. . . .

There was a charge that a ton of hay had been stolen from another farmer named Rossner and the court, after quiet was restored, wanted to know where that came in.

"Yo see, jedge," Jones said, "when my mother saw dat hoss she says he wa'nt nothin' but a bag o' bones, an' was jes' nachally dyin' on his feet. But I knew he was jes' hungry, an' there was that hay over on Rossner's farm, an'—well, that's all. Pears like I jes' had to have it, jedge."[15]

Dialect has its place in works of fiction but not in news articles, especially if it serves only to humiliate an individual and demean his or her entire race.

Reporters also gave women special attention in crime articles, though not to make fun of them or cite their character flaws. Some of the time reports cast women in the role of weak and fearful bystanders who happened to be near a crime and needed someone to protect them. On other occasions, reporters found them stepping out of this role and taking on a much more aggressive posture. In 1915 the *Boston Globe* described a woman pouncing on a would-be robber and wrestling with him while yelling at her husband to get out of the line of fire (the robber was armed). A few days later, the paper recounted a similar incident, which it headlined "Woman Beaten, Foiling Robbery."

Turn-of-the-century crime articles had more to say about race and ethnicity than would nowadays be considered appropriate. Papers did not hesitate to say derogatory things about minority offenders. On the other hand, they also had more laudatory comments for some offenders. These practices gave some color or flesh and blood to crime stories.

Whatever they had to say in describing offenders, they did not fear it would bring an avalanche of hostile letters to the editor. This was long before the civil rights movement and long before news media were chastised for reinforcing racial or ethnic stereotypes. At the time, Social Darwinism and its guiding motto, the survival of the fittest, were in full flower in America.

Newspapers often threw their spotlight in the direction of crime victims, noting their bleak condition and describing their feelings during or after the crime. Sometimes even doctors and relatives had a chance to comment. These stories often became quite detailed when dwelling on the plight of the victim:

[Dr. Deane] announced that the burns are not so deep as he first suspected, and he believes that he may be able to restore the girl's sight. At present, the girl's eyes are almost pure white in color from the acid burns, but owing to prompt medical attention the acid did not get a chance to penetrate far. The burns on the face, while at present very painful . . . will heal within a few days, and he hopes to obliterate all traces of the burns within a few months. . . .

Wilson spoke in no very optimistic way of his daughter's condition. He said: "The doctors give very favorable reports and state that they expect to save the sight of both eyes. But I am very much afraid that they are shooting hot air. . . .

"The effect of the acid must have been terrific. It burned clear through her clothes, and the few spatters that reached her hat burned away the straw like a red-hot iron."[16]

This crime, a spurned boyfriend throwing acid in the eyes of his former girlfriend, would probably make the newspapers today, but not in such detail. The report on the girl's condition would probably be condensed, with just a few sentences from the doctor's statement, and the father's opinion would not be solicited, let alone printed in full.

Witnesses too crept into crime news, particularly when their testimony proved central to the case. Newspapers sometimes devoted an entire article to them and often divulged the names and addresses of these witnesses, although in many instances suspicion fell on either the Mafia or the Black Hand. These organizations, if indeed they were responsible for the murders or assaults, no doubt welcomed this kind of information. Reporters thus put several witnesses in jeopardy, but apparently it did not occur to them or trouble their consciences for they continued the practice. Protecting one's sources was not valued then to the extent that it is today.

Reports often wove witnesses into the narrative as important characters taking part in an unfolding drama. The following account offers a taste of the heightened attention they received.

Simpson and Johanna Burke . . . were the principal witnesses [and this is their account]. Mrs. Cleary had been ill for some time and on the night of March 14th

Mrs. Burke went to see her. She met Simpson and his wife outside. The door was locked and Mrs. Burke told Simpson that Michael Cleary had said they were giving Mrs. Cleary some herbs which they got from the man over the mountains.

Voices could be heard from inside saying, "Take it, you witch!" and "Take it, you old faggot, or we will kill you."

When they finally gained admission they saw Dunne and three of the Kennedys holding Mrs. Cleary down on the bed with some decoction in a spoon. He called for some vile liquid, which was poured over the woman's body. A man on each side of the bed kept the body swinging about. The woman screamed horribly.[17]

In addition to the role of the witnesses, note the realism of the characters and action. The article goes far beyond supplying a few names, ages, and addresses.

In news stories written around 1900, reporters felt free to delve into personal lives and reveal people's thoughts and emotions. Famous people might receive such treatment but so did more ordinary citizens, particularly those central to a crime.

The prisoners were brought in by Sheriff George Helkes half an hour later, their faces bearing the marks of their wakeful forty hours during the deliberations of the jury. Mrs. Miller came in leaning on her husband's arm. Her eyes were red and she could scarcely contain her emotion as she walked across the courtroom. Dr. Miller's face showed the marks of sympathy because of his wife's sorrow.[18]

In attempting to read people's minds, this reporter had the advantage of being on the scene and seeing the people in person. Sometimes reporters tried to capture emotions and facial expressions without being there, indulging in poetic license to dramatize the victim's plight. Setting the scene and taking a point of view are techniques borrowed from fiction. Mailer, Capote, and Tom Wolfe have indulged in this kind of "new journalism." Actually, it is not new at all, for it was common in the days before objectivity came to be prized.

Dramatizing the case was especially common in murders. In a story headlined MUTILATED BODY TELLS OF A GHASTLY CRIME, the *San Francisco Chronicle* told of a victim whose dismembered trunk was left bleeding on a street corner; the body, armless, legless, and hacked to death, was still warm when it was discovered. The following day another banner headline: HEAD AND LIMBS FOUND TO FIT MAFIA VICTIM'S TRUNK. In addition to the main story, a sidebar told about the Lanteri boys, who found the missing parts floating near Fisherman's Wharf: "The Lanteri brothers untied the dark blue sock with which the sack was fastened and heedlessly delved into its contents. The sight which met their eyes would have shocked older nerves than theirs. With a yell of terror, the boys . . . tore up the bank and made for the tan shed."[19]

These early accounts relied on overstatement, often invoking terms such as "sensational" and "remarkable." They tried to make the events seem startling or the characters epic. When officials fought offenders, reporters would sometimes lapse into a Zane Grey style of writing.

[Sheriff] Matthews opened the door of the box car and was confronted by one of the robbers, who immediately presented a pistol and fired. Matthews was armed with a rifle. He returned the fire, the ball striking the robber near the point of a rib on the right side and going clear through him.

The robber then rolled over in the car and kept shooting at the officers, while his partner poked his pistol out of the car door and shot at Deputy Sheriff Nesbitt.

The officers returned fire, and two more bullets, one from Matthews' rifle and one from Nesbitt's pistol, struck the wounded man in the right knee. The other robber, when he saw his partner wounded, gave himself up and was taken to Scott's drug store, where he died at three o'clock this afternoon.[20]

This story contains logical impossibilities and several developments that strain credulity, but this is what passed for police reporting at the time. Reporters relied heavily on the police version and worried only about making it exciting, letting logic and facts take a back seat.

When describing crimes, many newspapers during the period between 1895 and 1915 offered blow-by-blow accounts. Sometimes readers had to wade deep into the story before reaching the crucial information. To assist them, papers supplied a cascading series of little headlines for the longer articles. Without such clues, a reader would have to follow the plot and wait while the mystery built. The following, which I have shortened considerably, is an excerpt from one such story.

A girl with fluffy, golden hair, who might have served as a model for a magazine cover, sat at a rear table in Natalby's Randolph street restaurant yesterday afternoon, nervously fingering her handbag. She was waiting for someone.

At the door stood Joseph Schmitt, the head waiter. He, too, was waiting. . . . Presently the person expected arrived—a woman followed by two small children. She wore jewels and clothing that strikingly set off her beauty. . . . Leaving the children at the door the woman made her way through the restaurant. She sank into a chair opposite the girl. Obviously, she was angry. . . .

"Why don't you leave Everett alone? He is nothing to you. You are trying to steal him. I know!" The girl snapped open her handbag. Out flashed a small revolver. From the bull-dog muzzle leaped a stab of flame. With a shriek the other woman jumped from her chair.

"I'm shot! She's killed me!" she screamed as she fled between the tables and out into Randolph street. . . . The girl with the golden hair had fainted, still clutching the revolver. She opened her eyes a few minutes later to see a traffic policeman bending over her. Then she became hysterical.[21]

Probably the most attractive characteristic of newspapers long ago was their use of narrative instead of the inverted pyramid. This meant that (unlike news articles of today) readers could not stop after a paragraph or two. Stories such as the one about the blonde woman began with paragraphs that enticed readers to follow it to the end and find out what finally happened—for this was not revealed in the introduction. Reporters thus used narrative with considerable success, especially when the subject was light or offbeat.

The story above really was a story; modern news items are not. Nowadays reporters stress objectivity and employ the inverted pyramid, which forces them to let facts dribble out in descending order of importance and effectively kills any suspense the story might have had. Thus, for instance, if "Dan Rather were telling the story of Little Red Riding Hood, he would say, 'Good evening. Last night a wolf ate a grandmother. Now here's Marilyn Berger to give you the rest.' "[22]

In summary, news articles around the turn of the century did not reflect a muckraking tradition, for crime news did not attract very aggressive reporting. Journalists did not describe criminal offenders as savage beasts nor imply that they deserved the most severe punishment possible. They did not normally depict crimes as part of a wave threatening to destroy the rest of society. Reporters who investigated crimes were not carrying on a crusade to rid the city of predators. In this sense, at least, the temperocentrists are correct: crime reporting in the olden days was not attack journalism.

A real test of the temperocentrist argument, however, cannot stop with crime news. Their argument focuses not on crime but on politics and how it was and is reported. They insist that journalists in recent years have treated presidents cruelly. Historical research, on the other hand, shows that the political press of the current era has been kinder and gentler by far than in the early years of the republic, when bombastic invective reached an all-time high (or, perhaps, low). It was then that the *Washington Monitor*, for example, complained that "the popular taste becomes vitiated and is prepared to receive the pestilential banquet of every noxious creature that wields a pen."[23]

Today's reader knows of George Washington in part from the writing of Parson Weems, who tried to make him a saint. During Washington's presidency, however, the newspapers did not hesitate to vilify him. Thus, one Philadelphia paper ran a long editorial, the essence of which was: "If ever a nation was debauched by a man, the American nation was debauched by Washington."[24] The five presidents who followed Washington did not find the reception much friendlier. Thomas Jefferson, to cite one example, gave the press the most stirring defense since John Milton, but the press gave him so much rhetorical abuse that it caused him to suffer severe headaches and depression, forcing him to stay in his room for days at a time.

Newspapers accused him of maintaining a black servant as his mistress, selling his slave-born children, seducing the wife of his best friend, and being an atheist. The *Connecticut Courant* warned its readers to watch out for their homes, parents, wives, and children in case Mr. Jefferson ever got near them. "Are you prepared to see your dwellings in flames, hoary hairs bathed in blood, female chastity violated, or children writhing on the pike and the halbert?"[25]

Passions aroused by the Civil War led the press to harass Abraham Lincoln, and it comes as no surprise that southern newspapers led the assault. The *Charleston Mercury*, for instance, called him a "horrid-looking wretch," "sooty and scoundrelly in aspect, a cross between . . . the horse swapper and the night man, a creature fit evidently for petty treason." After Lincoln was assassinated, a Houston paper said, "From now until God's judgment day, the minds of men will not cease to thrill at the killing. . . . It goes upon that high [honor] roll for nations and for universal man, with the slayings of [Charles I and Marat]." Northern papers could be equally harsh. The *Chicago Times* called him a "noisome stench thrust under the nostrils of the community," while the *New York Herald* labeled Lincoln's men as "the most disgraceful exhibition of human depravity ever witnessed."[26]

No other president matched Lincoln in the sheer amount of press hostility; Grover Cleveland, though, was perhaps first runner-up. As a young man he fathered a child out of wedlock. Later, after he had married another woman, he continued providing regular support for the child, but when he ran for the presidency, the press resuscitated the old story and pursued Cleveland with a vengeance, calling him a rake, a libertine stained with disgusting infamy. The man who followed Lincoln into the White House also received cutting blows, the most memorable from the *New York World*. It called him "an insolent brute in comparison with whom Caligula's horse was respectable."[27] This, of course, was Andrew Johnson.

By contrast, the press has not had the temerity to treat Nixon or Johnson (Lyndon, that is) this harshly. Many commentators persist in believing that the media hounded Johnson into early retirement by undermining public support for the war in Vietnam. Television brought the war into people's living rooms, according to Marshall McLuhan, and the more they saw of it the less they liked it. But this argument fails to take into account several important considerations. At the outset and for years following, television reporters and commentators were hawkish, portraying the war as morally correct and militarily winnable.[28]

Johnson's political fortunes took a sudden turn for the worse when Eugene McCarthy, the little-known antiwar candidate, did much better than anticipated in the New Hampshire primary. He did not actually win (getting only 42 percent of the votes), nor did Johnson lose, for he was not on the ballot and thus had to be written in; but the results were widely interpreted as a public repudiation of Johnson's war policy. They may have been, but it does not follow that watching the nightly news made New Hampshire residents pacifists and doves. Three-fifths of McCarthy's votes came from those who wanted to pursue the war more aggressively.[29] People whose first preference was all-out war did not automatically opt second for Johnson's limited war. Many felt America should either win or get out.

Television played practically no role in the Korean War, but that war followed essentially the same pattern as the one in Vietnam: early support dwindled as American casualties mounted. Usually, when the costs of war rise, the popularity of the president erodes. Johnson found his image deteriorating over time just as Harry Truman's had, and both men decided not to run for reelection. Nixon won the 1968 election, just as Eisenhower had in 1952, with a promise to clean up the mess in Asia.[30]

It is true that television covered the antiwar movement, but not in a way that won over many to the cause. Protesters acquired an image as people with long hair and scruffy clothes who burned their draft cards and the American flag. Some declared their support for Ho Chi Minh. They said Vietnam was experiencing a civil war and intervention by the United States was unwarranted and profoundly immoral. Eventually, a large portion of the American public became disenchanted with the war but not for these reasons. Instead they concluded that such a war was too costly, in American lives and money. The antiwar protesters so alienated Americans generally that Nixon ran against the movement and won easily.[31]

Once in office, he continued the war for several years. News media failed to undermine war support, for in November 1969 Nixon won approval of his war policy from 77 percent of Americans in a Gallup poll. In the 1972 election, George McGovern based his campaign on opposition to the war, and the resulting defeat ended his career. This evidence indicates that the press did not encourage antiwar sentiment.

CONCLUSION

Unlike the surveillance argument, the temperocentrist view has to do with style. Part diatribe and part nostalgia, the temperocentrist view says today's reporters are nasty, aggressive, and hard-hitting in contrast to the gentle souls of journalism's past. Actually, there is considerable evidence that the press of yore was not nearly so well mannered as temperocentrists say. The nineteenth century began with what is known as the dark ages of journalism and ended with yellow journalism. The gloves were taken off then and, according to historians, newspapers were shrill, savage, raucous, virulent, screaming, spiteful, and sententious. Temperocentrists who say reporting in the past was gentle reveal their innocence of history.

If they directed their argument at crime news instead of political news, they would have a stronger case, for crime articles of the past did not resemble muckraking exposés; they were more likely to appeal to readers by noting the offenders' good points and by building up to a dramatic climax. Reporters sometimes put more effort into making a story interesting than in making it accurate; Mencken and his colleagues made up names, ages, addresses, and biographies of victims when finding the real ones posed too much of a bother. Making crimes into human-interest stories precluded muckraking, investigative journalism for the most part. Newspaper reporters left that to the magazine writers.

According to the functionalist surveillance argument, newspapers are a distant early warning system. Crime articles alert officials that crime is on the rise. Conversely, when rates are low, papers print fewer crime articles, because there is no need for warnings. Front-page news stories drawn from the *Boston Globe, Chicago Tribune,* and *San Francisco Chronicle* for 1895 to 1915, however, cast doubt on this theory: crime *rates* were low in this period but crime *news* flourished. Why does the theory fail? First of all, editors do not set out to reflect trends in crime (or other areas of activity). They remain largely unaware of trends, because the news business encourages tunnel vision, a concentration on the narrowly recent (the past 12 or 24 hours). Second, the size of the news hole remains constant and must be filled whether the news day is busy or slow. Thus crimes may make the front page whether or not they are great in some absolute sense. Editors adjust to what they have.

There is a third reason why the surveillance argument fails. This is what we might call Lane's anomaly: the rarer something is, the more newsworthy it becomes. This is the point of Roger Lane's comment about the Bronx robbery back in the 1890s. It could have made the front page in a Philadelphia paper only if it were unusual. If it were not a rare occurrence, the paper would have had no reason to print it.

That the functionalist surveillance argument fails should come as no surprise to criminologists. For some years, textbooks in the field have insisted that there is no relationship between the amount of crime occurring in some jurisdiction and the amount of crime news in the local papers. They had only one study to cite (F. James Davis's study of four Colorado newspapers), but it appears that they were correct.[32] It may also be true that these days public officials take crime news with a grain of salt. That is, when more crime appears in the news, officials do not automatically assume that the actual rate of crime has risen. This question, however, remains to be studied. If we find that officials do not respond, that would be more evidence that crime news has become a paper tiger and not a distant early warning system.

NOTES

1. John Maynard Keynes, *The General Theory of Employment, Interest and Money* (New York: Harcourt, Brace, 1935), p. 383.

2. Albert Biderman, Louise Johnson, Jennie McIntyre, and Adrienne Weir, *Report on a Pilot Study in the District of Columbia on Victimization* (Washington, D.C.: Government Printing Office, 1967).

3. Carol Memmett, "Percentage of Households Touched by Crime Is Stable," *USA Today*, June 12, 1989, p. 8A.

4. Sir Leon Radzinowicz and Joan King. *The Growth of Crime* (New York: Basic Books, 1977), p. 6.

5. Henry Stokes, "In Japan, Crime Is Rare," *New York Times*, April 12, 1981, p. E7.

6. Morris Lurie, "In the Safest City in the World," *New York Times*, November 24, 1979, p. 23.

7. "U.S. Says Violent Crime Dropped from '80 to '84," *New York Times*, May 9, 1988, p. A15; "Europeans Steal More While U.S. Citizens Prefer Violence," *Crime Control Digest* 22 (May 1988): 6.

8. Richard Maxwell Brown, *Strain of Violence* (New York: Oxford University Press, 1975), pp. 35–36.

9. Roger Lane, "On the Social Meaning of Homicide Trends in America," in *Violence in America*, ed. Ted Robert Gurr, (Newbury Park, CA: Sage, 1989), p. 68.

10. J. Edgar Hoover, *Uniform Crime Reports* (Washington, D.C.: Department of Justice, 1971); William Webster, *Uniform Crime Reports*, (Washington, D.C.: Department of Justice, 1981).

11. Lane, "On the Social Meaning of Homicide Trends in America," p. 55.

12. Michael Robinson, "Fifty Years in the Doghouse," *Washington Journalism Review* 8 (March 1986): 44–45.

13. David Halberstam, *The Powers That Be* (New York: Dell, 1979).

14. "Robbers Still Free," *San Francisco Chronicle*, April 1, 1895, p. 1.

15. " 'Lynchers' Force Boy to Confess," *Chicago Tribune*, April 15, 1915, p. 1.

16. "Police Comb Bay Counties in Vain for the Assailant of Ruth Frances Wilson," *San Francisco Chronicle*, April 14, 1910, p. 1.

17. "Burned as a Witch,"*San Francisco Chronicle*, April 5, 1895, p. 1.

18. "Miller Is Guilty; Mrs. Saylor Also," *Chicago Tribune*, April 11, 1910, p. 1.

19. "Missing Members Found by Boys," *San Francisco Chronicle*, April 7, 1905, p. 1.

20. "Battle with a Robber," *San Francisco Chronicle*, April 4. 1915, p. 1.

21. "Shoots at 'Other Woman' in Loop Cafe, But Misses," *Chicago Tribune*, April 9, 1915, p. 1.

22. Don Fry, *Believing the News* (St. Petersburg, FL: Poynter Media Institute for Media Studies, 1985), p. 137.

23. John Tebbel, *The Media in America* (New York: Crowell, 1974), p. 88.

24. Ibid., p. 79.

25. Paul Boller, Jr., *Presidential Campaigns* (New York: Oxford University Press, 1984), p. 12.

26. Ibid., p. 107; Herbert Mitgang, *Abraham Lincoln: A Press Portrait* (Chicago: Quadrangle Books, 1971), pp. 476–477; Justin Walsh, *To Print the News and Raise Hell* (Chapel Hill: University of North Carolina Press, 1968), p. 196.

27. Joseph Spear, *Presidents and the Press* (Cambridge: MIT Press, 1984), p. 36.

28. Daniel Hallin, *The Uncensored War* (New York: Oxford University Press, 1986).

29. Lawrence Wright, *In the New World* (New York: Knopf, 1986), p. 129.

30. Michael Mandelbaum, "Vietnam: the Television War," *Daedalus* 111 (Fall 1982): 166.

31. John Tebbel and Sarah Watts, *The Press and the Presidency* (New York: Oxford University Press, 1985); Edwin Emery and Michael Emery, *The Press and America* (Englewood Cliffs, NJ: Prentice-Hall, 1984).

32. F. James Davis, "Crime News in Colorado Newspapers," *American Journal of Sociology* 57 (January 1952): 325–330.

Chapter Three

Dysfunctions

If, as previous chapters suggest, crime news has no beneficial effects, perhaps it has harmful ones. This idea has been advanced by more than a few commentators. Sociologist John Conklin, for instance, concludes ruefully that crime costs society in many ways. People may avoid the streets and put a police lock on their front door. They may avoid local libraries and schools at night. They may decide not to attend meetings of social groups or volunteer organizations. Or they may take more aggressive steps, such as carrying a gun, installing a burglar alarm, or hiring security guards.

Conklin believes that people's perceptions of crime depend partly on what they see in the news: the more crime sprawled across the news, the more they tremble.

People are now aware of the news more quickly, which makes them become better informed but also more apprehensive about events such as crimes and riots. The media have increased the number of threat messages. . . . Media reporting of crime is immediate, dramatic, and free of historical perspective and therefore leads to exaggerated fear of crime.[1]

Commentators complained for years about the ill effects of mass media, usually citing fictional rather than news programs and particularly objecting to violence shown to children, who are thought most susceptible to influence. This chapter will begin by summarizing some theories of media dysfunctions, then consider more specifically the possible dysfunctions of crime news.

SEDUCTION OF THE INNOCENT

The first commentator to stress how badly the mass media harmed children was psychiatrist and neurologist Frederic Wertham. We might expect worries of this kind to involve a medium that children could hear or could watch passively, such as radio, movies, or television, but Wertham chose a different source of mischief. Upon interviewing children with emotional problems at his mental hygiene clinics located in Harlem and other parts of New York City, he learned about comic books and their supposedly devastating impact.

According to Wertham, of the various kinds then being manufactured, crime comics were the most pernicious and the most popular. He said that in 1954, for instance, 60,000,000 comic books were sold in America, and most were devoted to crime. Apparently such comics held a special appeal for children, for Wertham found them everywhere, including his own clinics. Children would pore over them for a day or two and then sell them to the next eager customer (so readership greatly exceeded initial sales). Crime comics relied on three motifs (horror, science fiction, and the supernatural) and three common settings (urban, western, and jungle). And their content, apparently unbeknownst to most parents, gravitated toward the prurient.

Jungle comics [for instance] specialize in torture, bloodshed and lust in an exotic setting. Daggers, claws, guns, wild animals, well- or over-developed girls in brassieres and as little else as possible, dark "natives," fires, stakes, posts, chains, ropes [and] Nordic he-men dominate the stage. They contain such details as . . . white men banging natives around; a close-up view of the branded breast of a girl; a girl about to be branded.

I feel like a fool to have to prove that this kind of thing is not good mental nourishment for children.[2]

Wertham said that crime comics interfered with children developing a conscience and affected all children, not just the deprived or delinquent. Children who read crime comics identified with active, successful, dominating characters no matter how immoral they were. Comic books, Wertham said, did not educate children in the conventional sense but taught them to lie, cheat, and steal (even how to conceal the evidence). While the covers consistently proclaimed that crime does not pay, comics conveyed the opposite message on all picture frames but the last.

To buttress his claim that crime comics lead youngsters to become immersed in delinquent behavior, Wertham relied on clinical, anecdotal, and speculative evidence. By filling his book with accusations and lurid examples and bringing to light only the sinister aspects of the comic industry he made it clear that he was campaigning to sway public opinion. Wertham carried a simple message: crime comics override family, church, and school influences, causing a mass conditioning of children. While this message failed to convince many psychologists, sociologists, and criminologists, it attracted a strong following among the American public. In some ways, Wertham's crusade succeeded beyond all expectations.

Local organizations secured ordinances in eighteen states restricting the sale of crime comics. The General Federation of Women's Clubs, the American Legion, the Junior Chamber of Commerce, and countless other organizations pressed an attack on the comic publishing industry. Perhaps the most far-reaching effect of this movement was the decision of the Senate subcommittee on delinquency to investigate the comics industry.[3]

Soon afterward most publishers of crime comics closed shop, thus making Wertham's policy hopes a reality. But where his plans succeeded, his thesis failed, for after crime comics disappeared from the marketplace, juvenile delinquency showed no signs of withering away. Indeed, by most accounts, it reached new heights.

CHILDREN AND TELEVISION

Because criminologists and delinquency theorists nowadays consider Wertham's thesis ludicrous, they do not include any references to it in delinquency books. But a somewhat parallel idea has emerged and seems to have attracted considerable attention, namely, that children are influenced adversely by watching television programs. Research has particularly focused on the increased aggressiveness in children that is said to follow exposure to television.

This issue has attracted a flurry of research and commentary, including several major government reports. Most of the summaries have tended to exaggerate the extent to which television influences children, perhaps because the people who wrote them were committed to the thesis that television has important impacts. When the results reach popular magazines and newspapers, they may be further overstated. Thus these articles must be discounted somewhat because of the bias and enthusiasm of the writers. Such caveats aside, however, there is apparently some link between watching television and what children think and do.

In one of the more revealing studies, researchers compared three Canadian communities, Notel, Unitel, and Multitel. At first, Notel had essentially no television reception, while Unitel received one station and Multitel four. In other respects, the towns were pretty similar. Researchers chose the three as part of a natural experiment. They knew that later Notel would begin receiving one station's signals. In phase one, they studied children in grades four and seven; in phase two they came back two years later and looked at the same kids in grades six and nine and another group in grades four and seven. Thus they could compare the same children at different times, different ages at the same time, and children from different towns.

The researchers found a relationship between television watching and reading skills, which they attributed to the fact that reading is more demanding and less rewarding than watching the tube. They also found that television discourages the growth of creativity. It displaces other activities that might encourage creative thinking or problem solving. Most important, though, television affects aggression. After television arrived in Notel, there was a significant rise in aggressive behavior, regardless of sex, age, type of aggression (physical or verbal), and initial level of aggressiveness.[4] Why this effect occurred remains uncertain, however, though a number of theories have been proposed. More important for our purposes, though, is what effects media have on adults.

HYPODERMIC NEEDLE

The first attempt to explain media effects was the hypodermic needle theory. This theory was a by-product of the idea of mass society, a term used to describe the social changes that urbanization, modernization, and industrialization had upon individuals. Nineteenth-century sociologists contended that modernization threatened to sever the ties of human relationships between friends and relatives. As the world underwent rapid social change, people began moving to the cities and leaving their communities behind.

Social theorists held a romantic view of small-town and rural life in the distant past, imagining it as an idyllic setting where peace, harmony, and warm hospitality reigned. In the villages of old, kinship and church gave rise to ritual, respect, tradition, and ties of deep commitment to the community.

In contrast to this idealized view of the past, early sociological thinkers described life in the modern city in bleaker terms: community life disintegrated, and people became atomistic and alienated individuals who lacked primary-group (that is, intimate) ties and stabilizing traditions. What relations they had with others were mostly tenuous or specialized (like rider and driver or clerk and shopper). In the city, individuals became not only withdrawn, confused, and unattached but also susceptible to totalitarian movements and mass persuasion via propaganda. Voters, buyers, and spectators became an easy-to-appeal-to homogeneous mass. As Albert Hunter noted, "A specter is haunting the rise of mass society, the specter of the isolated, alienated urbanite, uprooted, roaming unattached through the streets of the city, a perpetual stranger."[5] Theorists said that community declined, and because of that there arose a mass society of alienated individuals.

Without traditional frames of reference supplied by family, friends, church, or village, people became much more malleable. It became apparent during World War I that they were susceptible to propaganda. The Great War required that soldiers be mobilized; industries be converted; production be increased; and people change jobs, organize to defend their homeland, and do without staples to which they had grown accustomed. Government officials decided that such a massive reorganization of society could not be carried out using ordinary means. A propaganda campaign would have to be mounted.[6] It was undertaken and apparently proved successful. Even people today who were born long after the war know some of the campaign messages, such as the claim that Belgian babies were impaled on the bayonets of invading German soldiers.

The success of these atrocity stories and other World War I propaganda encouraged the creation of the hypodermic needle theory, which held sway during the 1920s and 1930s, and still appeals to people not well versed in mass communication research. According to this theory, mass media effects are uniform, direct, and powerful, because the stimuli are strong and the atomized audience receiving them is virtually powerless to resist. It is as if the messages were injected into the brain.

LIMITED EFFECTS

Theorists insisted that the mass media had a powerful impact on their audience, but researchers had some doubts about this, so they set out to measure the extent to which voters, buyers, and spectators were influenced by messages communicated by the media. In 1960, Joseph Klapper wrote *The Effects of Mass Communication*, which compiled the findings of hundreds of studies and put them in an overarching framework, marking a turning point in the field. Was persuasive mass communication an agent of change? Klapper said that for the most part it was not, that the most common result was constancy of opinion (which he called reinforcement), while minor change was next most common and conversion rarest. He cited several studies in this context, including the classic one by Lazarsfeld, Berelson, and Gaudet: *The People's Choice*. (The people were citizens of Ohio's Erie County, and their choice was whom to vote for in the presidential election of 1940.)

Those predisposed to vote for a particular party (and there were many) showed the keenest interest in the campaign; many of these individuals decided before the nominating conventions which party they would support. Others, lacking such a strong interest or beset by cross pressures, were initially uncommitted. Though they were expected to sway many voters, campaign oratory, propaganda, and advertising converted only 6 percent of those studied from one party to another during the campaign. The great majority chose a party before Roosevelt or Willkie was nominated and did not waver throughout the campaign. Listening to party propaganda merely confirmed their original intentions.[7]

According to Klapper, most people who attend to mass communications do not absorb all the messages or absorb any of them exactly as they are given: exposure, perception, and retention are all selective.

By and large, people tend to expose themselves to those mass communications which are in accord with their existing attitudes and interests. Consciously or unconsciously, they avoid communications of opposite hue. In the event of their being nevertheless exposed to unsympathetic material, they often seem not to perceive it, or to recast and interpret it to fit their existing views, or to forget it more readily than they forget sympathetic material.[8]

Unlike the hypodermic needle theorists who saw people as isolated atoms in a mass society, Klapper emphasized the influence of intimate groups; people join groups whose attitudes and opinions are congenial with their own. Continued good standing in the group makes them reluctant to change.

Many people are more influenced by opinion leaders than by the mass media. An opinion leader, who generally has a small following and leads on only one topic, say, politics, may be a friend, family member, or co-worker. He or she may be attentive to the mass media but selective in passing along information, for most of his or her leadership consists of keeping others in the group in line, not letting them stray into new or "deviant" thinking.

Klapper argued that the media have limited effects on their audiences, that most people are more readily influenced by friends and family members. The vast collection of studies he cited seemed to make his case a powerful, almost incontrovertible one. But he was writing at a time when not much was known about television. Maybe this new medium has altered the relationship between the sender and the receiver.

AFTER KLAPPER

In determining how valid the limited-effects model of Klapper and Lazarsfeld is, we might turn to political commercials, a growing presence on television these days. Millions of dollars are spent on such commercials during election campaigns, so we would expect them to have some impact on potential voters. But the most comprehensive study showed they have little: "As with television news, most speculation about televised political advertising has been mistaken. Despite the skilled propaganda techniques employed, advertising is not effective in manipulating voters. People are not taken in by advertising and hyperbole and imagery."[9]

With each new election comes an outpouring of opinion that the advertising won it. Bush trailed Dukakis by 17 points in the polls at one time, then surged ahead and won handily, an accomplishment attributed to strategists running the ad campaign. Some of the commercials accused Dukakis of being a card-carrying member of the ACLU. Others said he was soft on crime, because he let convicted murderer Willie Horton out on furlough, during which time Horton terrorized a Maryland couple. Preliminary analysis indicated that the public found most of the negative ads distasteful, but this has not prevented commentators from contending that Roger Ailes and his colleagues won the election for Bush with their television commercials. This viewpoint has many adherents, but there are some problems with it. For one thing, Ailes tried the same kind of strategy in other political races and did not fare so well. Second, the Bush victory can be explained without resorting to the influence of his ads.

In presidential elections, Republicans enjoy a 23-state advantage, the so-called "built-in lock." Democratic candidates for the presidency have not won in these states in the past five or six elections, so the tendency now is not even to campaign there as they are presumed unwinnable. Republicans need to win only a couple of big-population states in addition to these 23, and they have enough electoral college votes for a victory. Democrats have such a disadvantage in part because of their earlier support for civil rights legislation; most white males nowadays vote Republican in presidential elections. The other problem for Dukakis was that he was challenging an administration in a time of peace and prosperity. Such administrations are difficult to oust.

Finally, a close examination of the polls suggests that two events were crucial to the Bush success. The first of these was the Republican convention. In recent times, such conventions usually give the candidate a substantial boost in the polls, and this was no exception. After the convention, a series of polls by Gallup, the *Wall Street Journal*/NBC News, the *Washington Post*/ABC News, and others showed Bush's lead holding quite steady at four or five percentage points. This lead did not change until the second presidential debate, which an overwhelming number of Americans thought Bush won. After that point in the campaign, Bush's lead widened. Different organizations polling on the same day obtained different results, but in general the tallies during the period from the second debate to the day of the election showed Bush ahead by seven to nine points. On election day he won by eight points, that is, 54 percent to Dukakis's 46 percent. This does not prove that the political ads were irrelevant, but it suggests that the outcome of the election can be explained without referring to them.

SPIRAL OF SILENCE

One of the more recent challenges to the Klapper and Lazarsfeld limited-effects model has been proposed by German public opinion pollster Elisabeth Noelle-Neumann. She contends that most people are eminently social creatures in that they do not want to be isolated or to be ignored and avoided by their neighbors. People live in perpetual fear of separation and feel miserable when others turn away from them. It is this pronounced sensitivity to slight that renders humans so susceptible to influence. They watch their environment closely to determine which way the winds of opinion are blowing, which are on the rise and which are on the wane.

Even isolated people are alert to signals and hence able to sense how the tide is turning on important issues and political contests. Swings in popularity are detected everywhere at about the same time and by all population groups. People who find their own views in the ascendant tend to express themselves openly; according to Noelle-Neumann, this includes such gestures as wearing a campaign button, putting a bumper sticker on one's car, and carrying a partisan newspaper where it can be seen easily. But people who think their views are unpopular will conceal them and keep quiet. Because one group expresses itself "with self-confidence whereas the others remain silent, the former appear to be strong in public, the latter weaker than their numbers suggest. This encourages others to express themselves or to fall silent, and a spiral process comes into play."[10]

Journalists are constantly searching for the new, unusual, changing, and surprising, because that is the nature of the "news" business. They bring what they find to the attention of their audience. Television viewers are bombarded with these messages and cannot be as selective in what they attend to as newspaper readers (who, after all, can skip any article they wish not to read). This makes television a powerful medium, Noelle-Neumann says, one that can change attitudes toward people and perceptions of the climate of opinion.

For instance, in recent West German elections, television journalists (who are generally more liberal than the rest of the country) tended to believe that the Christian Democrats had no chance to win. Their televised reporting helped convince the audience of this. People who watched these broadcasts then conveyed the same impression to the rest of the population, which emboldened supporters of the Social Democrats to speak out, while driving supporters of the Christian Democrats into a spiral of silence. In turn, this led to a last-minute swing in the voting, in which the Social Democrats won. Not wanting to be isolated, people followed the pack, which television journalists led to the left.

Ingenious and provocative, this analysis is also misguided. It implies that people have no close ties to friends, family, or other reference groups. Instead they orient themselves and their thinking to society as a whole. It also implies that people are acutely sensitive to minor statistical changes in public opinion and that all beliefs are lightly held. These assumptions are regarded as highly dubious by other sociologists and public opinion researchers. Furthermore, Noelle-Neumann's analysis does not seem to fit the American situation very accurately. For example, Harry Truman was given virtually no chance to win by pollsters and journalists in 1948 but he did anyhow.

For the 1984 presidential election campaign, Michael Robinson followed the television news presentation of candidates during September and October, paying special attention to the relationship between spin factor (innuendos and comments about the candidates' abilities to serve in high office) and candidate popularity. For Ferraro, the correlation between spin and popularity week by week was $-.33$, indicating that when her media image was most positive, her standing with the public was plummeting. For Mondale, the correlation between spin and popularity was $-.07$, and for Bush $+.18$, both of these correlations weak enough to suggest that spin has a negligible impact. While spin and public image did correlate positively for Reagan, for those two months the media were mostly negative and his public favorability scores consistently positive.

Robinson wondered what made viewers impervious to news spin about candidates. For one thing, he suggested, the media do not generally cast their lot with this candidate or that and deprecate the other candidates. Despite accusations of partisanship, television stories on campaigns have a distinctly liberal or conservative slant in less than 3 percent of the cases. In addition, their verbs are not insinuational nor are their adjectives pejorative.

Robinson suggested that incumbents perhaps have always had to endure a tougher press than challengers, but this handicap has not prevented them from winning reelection. In the broadcast era of 1932 onward, only one president up for reelection has lost (Carter). In the years before 1932, incumbents did not fare so well. This suggests that radio and television spin matters little when compared with events and conditions such as war and the economy.[11]

CULTIVATING

Like Noelle-Neumann, George Gerbner and his associates at the Annenberg School of Communications at the University of Pennsylvania regard the typical television viewer as isolated and atomized. Gerbner and his people, however, believe that television leads viewers to accept a right-wing police state. They claim that prime-time entertainment programs are especially powerful, in part because they present the same messages over and over.

Never before have such large and varied publics—from the nursery to the nursing home, from ghetto tenement to penthouse—shared so much of the same cultural system of messages and images, and the assumptions embedded in them. . . .

Imagine a hermit who lives in a cave linked to the outside world by a television set that functioned only during prime time. His knowledge of the world would be built exclusively out of the images and facts he could glean from the fictional events, persons, objects, and places that appear on TV. His expectations and judgments about the ways of the world would follow the conventions of TV programs, with their predictable plots and outcomes.[12]

Gerbner maintains that viewers are unselective, that is, they turn on television at a particular time and watch whatever program is playing at the moment.

According to Gerbner's cultivation theory:

1. Television is the most pervasive medium in American culture; the role it plays is historically unprecedented.

2. Television acts as an agency of the established order by cultivating norms, values and beliefs that uphold the present socio-politico-economic system instead of critiquing it.

3. Television permeates all ages and classes; no community is immune to its influence. Hence, disparate groups now share the same perspectives and consciousness.

4. It monopolizes the thinking of the third of American adults who watch it an average of at least four hours a day. The more time they spend viewing it, the more likely they are to perceive the world the way it does.

5. Night-time television is teeming with violent confrontations, and most prime-time characters engage in violent acts.

6. Their diet rich in televised violence, viewers integrate this into their thinking: viewing the world as a mean, scary, dangerous place.

7. This fear causes whites to flee the cities, brings more calls for police protection, and leads people to vote for law-and-order candidates who promise order via force.[13]

According to research Gerbner cites, heavy viewers are more likely than light viewers to overestimate the number of males employed in law enforcement and to say that:

people cannot be trusted

people look out for themselves

the lot of the average person is getting worse

officials do not care about the public

things are so bad it would be unfair to bring a child into the world now

there is a high probability that they will become victims of violence at any given time.

Some commentators disagree with this. One critic of television said that it has the opposite effect, that is, teaching that things always turn out well in the end. Thus, there is dispute over what the television view of reality is. In addition, the relationships Gerbner cites are modest: heavy viewers differ from light viewers by 10 percent or less on the items he stresses. Differences so small hardly deserve a second look, let alone an elaborate theory and ominous warnings about the fall of civilization. The differences, already minimal, diminish further when age, sex, and education of respondents are statistically controlled (as they need to be, since heavy viewers tend to be older, female, and less educated). Finally, other researchers have noted that, contrary to Gerbner's theory, nonviewers are consistently more fearful than light viewers, and extremely heavy viewers are less fearful than heavy viewers.[14]

Other researchers have examined the issue of whether television viewing increases fear of crime but few find support for Gerbner's theory. Doob and MacDonald found more fear among people who watch more television and more violent programs, but only among people who live in high-crime areas. They concluded that fear caused people to watch more television—not the reverse.[15] Sacco discovered a very small correlation between television watching and fear of crime; after he statistically controlled for age, sex, and social class, it decreased further.[16] Using national data, O'Keefe found exposure to television in general, to television crime news, and to television crime entertainment practically unrelated to all of the following:

1. perception that crime in the neighborhood is rising
2. feeling unsafe alone at night in the neighborhood
3. viewing one's neighborhood as more dangerous than others
4. believing one's residence will be burgled
5. believing that one will be attacked or robbed
6. evaluating police and courts performance
7. wanting criminals punished to the maximum
8. wanting more police on the streets

9. thinking crime is inevitable

10. anomie; altruism; trust in people[17]

These researchers are not alone. Skogan and Maxfield said that viewing crime on television has no effect on fear.[18] An important Canadian study found that watching television does not produce fearful or negative attitudes toward the outside world. "The most conservative interpretation, and the one we favor, is that television has no influence [on adult behavior and attitudes]."[19]

NEWSPAPERS AND CRIMINALS

In recent decades the search for media effects has centered on television, for theorists have thought it to be the most powerful medium. Researchers have discovered, however, that its effects are weaker than anticipated. Not much has been said about the effects of newspapers; this may be because theorists have not argued much about them. Or it may be that researchers have looked into the question and found their effects even weaker than those of television. But since this book is about newspapers, we should at least consider the question.

Doris Graber has taken up the issue. She looked at how the *Chicago Tribune* and its readers view the causes of crime and the nature of criminals. If the strong media theories are correct, the *Tribune* and its readers should see eye-to-eye on these. (In another study, Bob Roshier did not find readers and their papers to be in agreement about crime, but since his study took place in England, critics could argue that the findings are inapplicable to the United States.)[20]

Ninety-five percent of those Graber studied said that the media are their primary sources of information about crime, but this does not mean that the media are relied upon when respondents make judgments and interpretations about crime. Readers have other resources to tap for these, such as friends and co-workers, spouses and other relatives, personal experiences and convenient stereotypes. Furthermore, media crime stories ordinarily shun analysis and interpretation. As a rule, crime stories do not hazard a guess at what caused this crime in particular, and they are wary of mentioning the causes of crime in general or the remedies or punishments they think most apt.

The *Chicago Tribune* sometimes identified offenders by age, sex, and race; in those instances, they tended to be over 35, male, and white. When *Tribune* readers were asked to describe the typical offender, their picture matched the *Tribune*'s in one respect at least: they assumed most offenders to be men. Few readers (9 percent), however, believed the typical offender to be over 35, and fewer still saw him as white (See Table 4).[21]

When readers were asked of what occupational status they believed

Table 4
Criminals' Race and Age

	Tribune Data	Reader Estimates
Race		
Black	21.6%	61.4%
White	70.3%	7.4%
Latino	4.9%	4.4%
Other	3.2%	23.8%
Age		
Under 25	29.6%	47.6%
25 to 35	31.2%	43.6%
Over 35	39.1%	8.8%

most criminals to be, they typically did not mention a specific line of work but instead used such adjectives as poor, unemployed, and uneducated. In contrast, the *Tribune* itself, when mentioning occupations of offenders, identified 62 percent of them as bureaucrats, professionals, or business managers. The *Tribune* and its readers did not agree on the causes of crime either. The paper gave almost no consideration to causation, though on rare occasion it did assign blame, usually to the criminal justice system for being inefficient or lenient. Readers took another direction when asked about causation, citing poverty, economic stress, or unemployment.

When forming opinions about the nature of offenders and causes of crime, readers either forget or discount their newspaper. Graber says that people simply have fixed ideas about crime and criminals. These are based on personal experience or conventional wisdom and not readily altered by media exposure.

The topics of many of these stories have been covered for long periods of time, often ranging over the entire lifespan of adults. . . . Stories about these topics, therefore, are not genuinely "news" in the sense of something that has not happened before. They are episodes in a continuing story that simply reinforce what has been previously perceived as the main story theme. For such topics, people are likely to have developed conceptions about likely scenarios, causes, consequences. . . . These are not readily altered or replaced, irrespective of current media coverage, because rethinking and restructuring one's conceptions is a . . . painful task.[22]

Thus, people are not quite the lumps of clay that some theories imply; master propagandists cannot mold them at will. Despite the heroic efforts of the media, most people cling tenaciously to their own long-held views.

CONCLUSION

Classical sociological theorists described the problems of the modern era as social atomization, alienation, disorganization, and secularization. They helped fuel the critics of mass society, who argue that urbanization, modernization, and industrialization have had devastating effects on people and communities. According to these critics, as people moved to cities, they severed ties to family, friends, church, and village. Urban impersonality, loneliness, and isolation replaced these ties. While this thesis that modernization and urbanization undermine community has broad appeal, recent research shows that urban life has not caused a breakdown in community but the growth of plural communities based on ethnicity, occupation, and style of life.[23] Urban living has not made close ties and intimate groups disappear.

Furthermore, researchers question whether people today have succumbed to the blandishments of mass media. Findings do not lend much weight to the premises of the hypodermic needle theory. Not long ago, for instance, William McGuire reviewed a monumental collection of research books, papers, and articles examining the nature and extent of media effects. When he published the findings and summaries of these 500 studies, there was no attendant publicity. He did not appear on talk shows or achieve overnight fame. Perhaps because his conclusion lacked excitement—most findings coincided with the null hypothesis that attending to media produces no consistent changes in people's values, beliefs, attitudes, or behavior.[24]

More apt to command public attention are theories claiming powerful media effects. Noelle-Neumann created a burst of excitement when she said that left-leaning news anchors on television inspire a spiral of silence among conservative members of the audience. Similarly, Gerbner received a surge of public attention when he claimed that people are cut off from one another and dependent on television for their outlook on life. Writers cited him copiously, implying that his arguments were beyond dispute; many studies, however, cast doubt on the dysfunctional effects he imputed to television.

We sometimes forget that theories are not religious revelations to be accepted on faith. No theory can be proved correct, for there is always the possibility that future data will demonstrate its weaknesses. Indeed, the only thing that can be proved about a theory is that it lacks validity, and that happens sooner or later to almost every theory in any science. Theories say A is related to B, B is related to C, C is related to D, and so on, and related in a certain way. Later these hypotheses are tested by using tests of significance, correlations, multivariate analysis or some other method. Unless the findings show the predicted relationships are strong and in the right direction, the hypotheses must be rejected. Thus it is that beautiful theories get shot down by ugly little correlations. This is as it should be, for we do not need a great many theories floating around, each with its devoted adherents. Inevitably, most, if not all of them, are not valid—they do not fit the available data. So it is with the functionalist and dysfunctionalist theories of the media.

NOTES

1. John Conklin, *The Impact of Crime* (New York: Macmillan, 1975), p. 22.

2. Frederic Wertham, *Seduction of the Innocent* (New York: Rinehart, 1954), p. 31.

3. James Gilbert, *A Cycle of Outrage* (New York: Oxford University Press, 1986), p. 106.

4. Leslie Joy, Meredith Kimball, and Merle Zabrach, "Television and Children's Aggressive Behavior," in *The Impact of Television*, ed. Tannis Williams (Orlando: Academic Press, 1986), p. 334.

5. Albert Hunter, "Persistence of Local Sentiments in Mass Society," in *Handbook of Contemporary Urban Life*, ed. David Street (San Francisco: Jossey-Bass, 1978), p. 134.

6. Melvin DeFleur and Sandra Ball-Rokeach, *Theories of Mass Communication* (New York: Longman, 1982), pp. 158–164.

7. Paul Lazarsfeld, Bernard Berelson, and Hazel Gaudet, *The People's Choice* (New York: Columbia University Press, 1948).

8. Joseph Klapper, *The Effects of Mass Communication* (Glencoe, IL: Free Press, 1960), p. 19.

9. Thomas Patterson and Robert McClure, *The Unseeing Eye* (New York: Putnam, 1976), pp. 22–23.

10. Elisabeth Noelle-Neumann, "Mass Media and Social Change in Developed Societies," in *Mass Media and Social Change*, ed. Elihu Katz and Tamas Scecsko (Beverly Hills, CA: Sage, 1981), p. 139.

11. Michael Robinson, "The Media in Campaign '84: Wingless, Toothless and Hopeless," in *The Mass Media in Campaign '84*, ed. Michael Robinson and Austin Ranney (Washington: American Enterprise Institute, 1985), pp. 34–39.

12. George Gerbner and Larry Gross, "The Scary World of TV's Heavy Viewer," *Psychology Today* 9 (April 1976): 42.

13. George Gerbner and Larry Gross, "Living with Television," *Journal of Communication* 26 (Spring 1976): 173–199; George Gerbner, Larry Gross, Marilyn Jackson-Beeck, Suzanne Jeffries-Fox, and Nancy Signorielli, "Cultural Indicators: Violence Profile No. 9," *Journal of Communication* 28 (Summer 1978): 176–207; George Gerbner, Larry Gross, Nancy Signorielli, Michael Morgan, and Marilyn Jackson-Beeck, "The Demonstration of Power," *Journal of Communication* 29 (Summer 1979): 177–196; George Gerbner, Larry Gross, Michael Morgan, and Nancy Signorielli, "The 'Mainstreaming' of America," *Journal of Communication* 30 (Summer 1980): 10–29.

14. Paul Hirsch, "The 'Scary World' of the Nonviewer and Other Anomalies," *Communications Research* 7 (October 1980): 403–456.

15. Anthony Doob and Glenn MacDonald, "Television Viewing and Fear of Victimization," *Journal of Personality and Social Psychology* 37 (February 1979): 170–179.

16. Vincent Sacco, "The Effects of Mass Media on Perception of Crime," *Pacific Sociological Review* 25 (October 1982): 475–493.

17. Garrett O'Keefe, "Public Views on Crime," in *Communication Yearbook*, ed. Robert Bostrom (Beverly Hills, CA: Sage, 1984), pp. 514–535.

18. Wesley Skogan and Michael Maxfield, *Coping with Crime* (Beverly Hills, CA: Sage, 1981).

19. Peter Suedfield, Brian Little, Dennis Rank, Darilynn Rank, and Elizabeth Ballard, "Television and Adults," in *The Impact of Television*, ed. Tannis Williams (Orlando: Academic Press, 1986), pp. 381–382.

20. Bob Roshier, "The Selection of Crime News by the Press," in *The Manufacture of News*, ed. Stanley Cohen and Jock Young (Beverly Hills, CA: Sage, 1981), pp. 28–39.

21. Doris Graber, *Crime News and the Public* (New York: Praeger, 1980), p. 56.

22. Doris Graber, *Processing the News* (New York: Longman, 1984), p. 76.

23. Claude Fischer, *To Dwell Among Friends* (Chicago: University of Chicago Press, 1982), p. 194.

24. William McGuire, "The Myth of Massive Media Impact," in *Public Communication and Behavior*, ed. George Comstock (Orlando: Academic Press, 1986), pp. 173–257.

Chapter Four

Omissions and Distortions

Research studies have found the "masses" not very compliant in the face of media messages, but, oblivious to the findings, "strong-media" enthusiasts continue to assert that the media exert a potent influence over audiences. Most proponents of this argument go on to identify other, more sinister aspects of the media, including biases in media messages or content. From Wertham to Gerbner, commentators have combined strong-media models with criticisms of the messages being transmitted.

The most prominent criticisms accuse the media of being too violent and too leftist. (While these are the most popular grounds for criticizing the media in recent years, they are rarely voiced by the same individuals; charges of violence come from one camp, those of leftism from a different one.) Chapters 5 and 6 will deal with the question of whether there is a leftist bias in the media. This chapter will discuss excessive violence, then move to other, perhaps more subtle, biases.

NEWS VALUES

What ingredients make an event or issue newsworthy depend on who makes the judgment. Editors from different papers have their own views and idiosyncrasies, which is why the *Washington Post* and *New York Times*, for instance, do not print the same front page stories. Journalism classes and textbooks have tried to breathe order into this newsroom anarchy by constructing lists of news values. Such lists inevitably vary from one to another, but the discrepancies are not very pronounced; by and large, the lists reflect a general consensus on what makes something suitable for printing. Here are some of the news values commonly cited:

Timeliness: Since readers want to know the latest information on the latest happenings, news should be new. According to the Chicago tradition, news reporters would walk over their grandmothers to reach a breaking story.

Conflict: Confrontations that interrupt society's serenity, such as war, riots, and killings, lend spice to people's days. News people have been known to contrive conflict where none really exists.

Novelty: Because people show more interest when events have an element of surprise, news media dwell on exceptional ones. This sets journalism in direct contrast to the social sciences, which search for consistent patterns.

Prominence: Celebrated, notorious, and highly placed figures make the news more often than the rest of the population, which is why *People* magazine exists and why the *National Enquirer* tends to emphasize such prominent people as Oprah Winfrey and Roseanne Barr.

Disaster: Destruction and catastrophe are big news. Many people turn on the radio first thing in the morning to hear if there are any earthquakes, wars, or assassinations to report.

Proximity: Events receive more attention if they have a local angle. For example, in November 1917, the *Bronx Home News* offered this headline: BRONX MAN LEADS RUSSIAN REVOLUTION. (Leon Trotsky once spent three months in the borough.)

Editors do not report every event that takes place in the world; nor do they cover a random or even "representative" sample of them. In general they favor events thought to contain the biggest conflict and have the greatest impact. In doing so, however, they present a distorted picture of the world, a picture that stresses spectacles over mundane events. Historically, crime news has given us two distortions in particular— choosing sides and Hearstian crimes. While these may not be as common now as they once were, they are worth noting.

Choosing Sides

News media have been known to describe the world, or a particular city, as brimming with conflict, suggesting that peace and tranquility are feeble and transitory states at best. A newspaper that acted otherwise would be quickly taken to task. In 1974, the *Boston Globe* gave school desegregation blanket coverage by sending out 48 reporters, one to each school, on the first day the new system took effect. Of these 48, all but one phoned in to say that things were quiet on the education front. To a non-journalist, the *Globe* did the sensible thing by noting how peaceably the day went. But it provoked a firestorm of protest, for *Time* magazine charged the paper with suppression, collusion, and censorship; by failing to trumpet conflict (no matter how atypical), the *Globe* apparently committed journalistic heresy.

While news media stress conflict, there are different kinds of conflict, and not all are valued equally. The kind they prefer differs from what the rest of society prefers. Ordinary people, when watching a game of soccer or football, or a boxing or wrestling match, prefer that the opponents be evenly matched, so that the winner remains in doubt for a long time, heightening the suspense. Similarly, if crimes must occur, the public wants the victim and offender to be of the same sex, size, and age. But the press prefers instead harrowing assaults by men against women, by young adults against the very young or the very old, and by large people against small and vulnerable targets.

When these one-sided crimes happen, the press emphasizes the obvious mismatch, the evil nature of the offender, and the goodness or innocence of the victim. When Carolyn Isenberg was raped and killed on a Manhattan rooftop, papers called her beautiful, bouncy, bright, courageous, dedicated, intelligent, likable, petite, remarkable, sensitive, talented, vivacious, and zestful. Her vices, if she had any, were never divulged. The offender, on the other hand, was described as a sneering, strutting killer. The cast is stereotypical, with a grieving family, a sinister criminal, and a saintly, martyred victim. The case is newsworthy because it is such a catastrophe; it is a catastrophe, however, only if the press makes the victim into a saint and the offender into a brute.

Hearstian Crimes

Crimes may be of the type mentioned above, that is, where the offender is big and strong and intent upon harm and the victim is small, weak, and innocent. Or they may be of the senselessly vicious type. The latter, aberrant kind of crime news story is sometimes associated with William Randolph Hearst, of whom it was once said that "when peace brooded over the city and nobody was being robbed or murdered, he would come down to the office with despondency written on his face."[1] Murders so invigorated him that he would dance around the page proofs.

Parts of a man's body, wrapped in oilcloth with a cabbage rose design, were fished out of the East River in the summer of 1897. They were assembled in the morgue, but with the head missing, identification was impossible. Hearst put his murder squad on the case, and they found out who the man was, where the oilcloth was bought, and what the woman buying it looked like. From this they were able to track her down. The victim was Willie Guldensuppe, and the murderer was his mistress. With a platoon of reporters on the case, Hearst kept it in the headlines for weeks.

Again it was the news values of conflict, novelty, and disaster that made the Guldensuppe case newsworthy. Readers exposed to this crime day after day for weeks or even months may have surmised that it was somehow typical or emblematic of crime in general. Most crimes, however, are not this lurid or heinous. Nor are they violent. Among those that are violent, few are murders. Of the murders, hardly any involve drowning and dismemberment beyond identification. Indeed, the typical crime is no more serious than the filching of an umbrella or a candy bar, one reason why people often forget they have been victimized.

PYRAMIDING

An inverted pyramid orders facts in an article by packing the most important ones into the first paragraph. Reporters then let details and matters of lesser import dribble out in later paragraphs, with the least important ones left for the last paragraph. This device saves both readers and editors. Readers can decide early on whether the story has anything in it of interest to them, and editors can lop off the bottom paragraphs without fear of excluding anything vital to the piece.

The inverted pyramid probably originated during the Civil War, when field correspondents were forced to depend on the telegraph to transmit their reports to papers at home. In that period, the telegraph system broke down often enough to cause dread and anxiety in many a correspondent; some breakdowns were caused by enemy troops, who simply cut the wires. Correspondents adapted to this vexing situation by turning to the inverted pyramid, that is, by compressing the most salient information into a few words at the beginning of their account. Thus, if the transmission were interrupted in the middle of the report, the crucial information would still get through.

The inverted pyramid stands as one of the centerpieces of journalistic objectivity, but it is grounded ultimately in subjectivity and value judgments. Every reporter, every newsroom, has computer terminals, desks, dictionaries, and other equipment and reference materials, but none of them has a master list of the most important facts—no handy guide to the modern version of the great chain of being. Reporters with a profusion of facts must decide on their own which ones have the greatest significance. This cannot be done without values intruding.

Inverted-pyramid writing not only allows values to creep in but invites and even insists upon them. The sociology of mass communication has long been missing an ideal opportunity to study values in the news, for it has not looked at which values are revealed by reporters and editors in their choice of facts to put in the first paragraph or two. One way to detect values revealed by the inverted-pyramid form is to contrast different papers' treatment of the same story. Consider, for instance, how various newspapers introduced Bernhard Goetz's surrender after he shot four teenagers and escaped to New Hampshire.

The *New York Times* gave the story a straightforward and unexceptional lead:

A Manhattan man surrendered to the Concord, N.H., police yesterday, saying he was the gunman who wounded four teen-agers on a subway car 10 days ago, police officials said.

They said the man, Bernhard Hugo Goetz, 37 years old, of 56 West 14th Street, had already been identified as a suspect in the shooting, which took place after the teen-agers approached him and asked him for money.[2]

Other papers, however, took advantage of the inverted-pyramid form to squeeze into the first two paragraphs many minor and dubious "facts." This is how the *Atlanta Constitution* reported the event:

A 37-year-old electrical engineer, accused of shooting four teenagers on a crowded subway after they allegedly tried to mug him, voluntarily surrendered to authorities Monday in Concord, N.H.

Dubbed the "Death Wish Gunman" and "The Subway Vigilante" by the city's splashy tabloids, the suspect was identified by police late Monday as Bernhard Hugo Goetz, a self-employed businessman whom neighbors described as a quiet, gentle, hard-working man who often led petition drives in the neighborhood's anti-crime campaigns.[3]

The *Constitution* tried to cast it in the mold of a preferred crime, that is, one with a pure, innocent, and defenseless victim and an offender who is the embodiment of evil (a difficult thing to do in this case, since Goetz did shoot all four teenagers, and no one actually mugged him). Thus the paper packed the first two paragraphs with information intended to make it seem as if there were a little bit of Mother Teresa lurking in Goetz's soul. This slant appeared in other papers, too, such as the *New York Post*, which opened its story by saying, "A Greenwich Village bachelor who was the target of muggers four years ago turned himself in yesterday as the subway vigilante in what police called an act of conscience 'to end the year on a good note.' "[4] This reporter's desperate search for facts to defend Goetz's actions takes him back four years to an event previously thought too insignificant to report (so much for timeliness as a news value).

SUPERFICIALITY

Now consider more typical cases, the kind that do not receive the intense coverage devoted to the Goetz saga. Normally, reporters write crime stories plainly, using precise and factual adjectives, giving the time and location of the crime, and isolating it from all other criminal incidents, in accordance with the first principle of objectivity. But by adhering to this rule, reporters may be ignoring the many important facts that lie below the surface. Reporters come along after the incident and see only the end result. Not knowing better, they may assume that the offender was a stranger who suddenly attacked the innocent victim for no reason (the classic assault).

Often, however, victims and offenders already know each other. Sometimes the victim does something to spur the offender into committing the crime. According to Marvin Wolfgang, quite a few homicides are victim precipitated—the victim strikes the first blow—especially in acrimonious marriages. The irate husband assaults his wife with, say, a brick or a bottle and she, standing there with a butcher knife in hand, does the thing that comes natural, she stabs him and he dies as a result. Even when they do not strike first, victims may hasten their own demise, as journalist Edna Buchanan notes in her comments on murder victims in Miami: "They deal drugs, steal, rob, or stray with somebody else's mate until a stop is put to them. They quarrel in traffic or skirmish over parking spaces with other motorists—who happen to be armed and short-tempered."[5]

OBJECTIVITY

If American journalism enjoys relatively high status in the present era, objectivity deserves some of the credit. In the early years of the republic, editors had no idea of what objectivity was. In the 1830s, the penny press broke away from rigid control by the political parties, but this did not end political partisanship in the press. Around the turn of this century, when Hearst and Pulitzer papers fought for circulation supremacy in New York, their example inspired yellow journalism's spread throughout the country, which aroused the ire of reformers, who deplored the yellows' excesses and called for more objective reporting. Wire services heard the call and applauded it, for by being nonpartisan they could sell to papers in different sections of the country and papers with different political ideologies.

But biases remained, because procedures designed to ensure objectivity did not always entail complete accuracy. Sometimes they hindered it, as in this example from television. In 1972, Nixon, unlike McGovern, felt no need to visit the hustings, so he stayed in the White House, where he could look presidential and achieve almost complete control over news about him. The one exception was Cassie Mackin, who charged him on several counts (as Timothy Crouse wrote):

She said: "On defense spending and welfare reform . . . there is a serious question of whether President Nixon is setting up straw men by leaving the very strong impression that McGovern is making certain proposals which in fact he is not."

She showed a film clip of Nixon saying: "There are some who believe . . . that it doesn't really make any difference whether the United States has the second strongest Navy, the second strongest Army, the second strongest Air Force in the world." Then Mackin said: "The President obviously meant McGovern's proposed defense budget, but his criticism never specified how the McGovern plan would weaken the country. On welfare, the President accuses McGovern of wanting to give those on welfare more than those who work, which is not true. On tax reform, the President says McGovern is calling for 'confiscation of wealth,' which is not true."[6]

The White House immediately pounced on NBC for airing such a statement. Stung by the rebuke, NBC did not defend its integrity or fight the pressure; instead it meekly submitted and sent Mackin off on what it euphemistically called reassignment. She came under fire not for any false statements but for not being sufficiently objective, a term that in the fraternity of journalists means

1. Reporters must write plainly, using precise, factual adjectives rather than ones carrying positive or negative connotations. They are required to record the exact time and location of an incident and isolate it from all others. They must avoid superlatives, lest they appear gushing or effusive.

2. They must report the facts they witness (that is, concrete, finite events rather than trends or general tendencies) and not interpret them. They must distinguish facts from values and remember that the latter belong on the editorial page only.

3. They should rely on statements from credible sources (which usually means sources in high government circles) and should not try to plumb their motives, for these cannot be inferred from outward appearances. Readers wanting conclusions will have to draw them on their own.[7]

These requirements put reporters under severe constraints. To gauge the depth of such constraints, perhaps we should ask journalists working on the *People's Daily* in Albania. Possibly, the strictures they face are not a great deal more insufferable than these.

SOURCING

Originally intended to reduce bias, these principles sometimes encourage it. The third one, for instance, constrains reporters to rely on powerful and highly visible people, who then try to impose their views. Herbert Gans calls these the Knowns, who may be political figures such as presidents, presidential candidates, people in Congress, or other high governmental officials. But relying on authorities is no more valid than the a priori method (I know it is true because it is self-evident) or the method of tenacity (I know it is true because I believe it with all my heart).

In the United States, where the president stands above all others in authoritativeness, whatever he says is taken as both accurate and printable. But presidents are not wholly reliable paragons of virtue. For one thing, despite their lofty status, they may not have at their fingertips the information they are asked about; often, aides and assistants are the ones who know the data much better than anyone else. Ronald Reagan has to be the ultimate example of the disengaged and uninformed chief executive. As he neared the end of his second term, some of his misstatements were revealed as false. The Tower Commission generously attributed them to ignorance and amnesia rather than to outright lying.

Other presidents have aroused more skeptical reactions. It is widely presumed that Lyndon Johnson lied to Congress about the Gulf of Tonkin incident, which he regularly used as the justification for the big military buildup in Vietnam. And Richard Nixon is thought to have lied repeatedly about his involvement in the Watergate cover-up. Indeed, Jimmy Carter won in 1976 in part by promising not to lie to the American people, which in ordinary times would be regarded as a minimum requirement for holding office instead of, in the post–Nixon years, a quaint virtue and formidable asset.[8]

Police, not presidents, act as sources in crime stories, but in the world of journalism police enjoy as much respect as anyone. Consider the phrase "police said." According to John Chancellor, "There are jokes in the business that you can write almost anything and get it past the editors as long as it is tagged with those two words. As in: 'The sky is falling, police said.' "[9] As the sole source of crime information, however, police have some serious drawbacks.

1. Police normally respond after a citizen calls the precinct and a dispatcher sends them to the address. There they interview victims and witnesses and may, in turn, pass this information (by now, thirdhand) on to reporters.

2. Most police have no college education or journalism training, so their questions rarely elicit the kind of facts journalists seek. Police probe those areas that are of interest to the department, not to the reading public.

3. Police, even if they uncover a treasure trove of interesting findings, are under no obligation to reveal it to the media. They may believe that a full reporting of what they know could tip off the offender and jeopardize the police effort.

4. Sometimes police bungle the case or abuse some innocent bystander. This will not come to light if police retain tight control over information. Reporters

who unctuously rely on police as sole sources may find their territory is being encroached upon.

5. Sometimes a crime cannot be understood without first delving into the histories of the victim and offender, but police rarely look into them. They prefer to think that crime depends on the defendant's character flaws, not on history, culture, social setting, or personal relationships.

6. Police investigate crimes, but not all varieties receive the same attention. Property crimes and violent crimes are reported to the precinct in great number, but crimes of business and other white-collar offenses do not provoke such a flood of calls. Indeed, they hardly provoke a trickle.

Relying on police because theirs is the official view steers reporters along a narrow trajectory, thereby inviting sample bias. Witnesses, victims, and suspects who could offer another side of the story get muted or silenced while the police voice is amplified. Traditional journalists teach students that nothing is true until the police confirm it. "Even if you pull a wallet from the victim's pocket, his identity must be confirmed by the police."[10]

REDLINING

The rules and conventions of objective journalism exhort reporters to depend on sources that are highly placed; conversely, they require that other possible sources—in particular, society's unknowns and have-nots—be ignored. Normally, the term "redlining" refers to such money lenders as bankers, figuratively drawing a line around old, run-down sections of the inner city and then denying loans and mortgages to individuals living there, even if they have sterling credit histories. Redlining may afflict the news business as well, as editors draw a line around the same area of the city and declare its people to be largely un-newsworthy.

As a young reporter in Chicago, Seymour Hersh once thought he had happened upon an important story: a man killed five people and then committed suicide. Hersh eagerly relayed this information over the telephone to the newsroom, where the long-time deskman asked him if the victims were black. When Hersh said that they were, the deskman immediately knocked the story down to a mere paragraph or two.[11] Chicago was not alone in the practice, as this excerpt from Russell Baker suggests:

Baltimore was as segregated racially as Johannesburg. Neighborhoods, schools, movie theaters, stores, everything was segregated. . . . [The *Sun*] covered practically no black news. Murders of black people were not "little murders." They weren't murders at all, as I discovered . . . on phoning the city desk with details of a man who had died of head injuries after being bludgeoned. "You can't hurt 'em by hitting 'em on the head," said the night editor, hanging up on me.[12]

New York Times reporters were advised not to phone in any killings in Harlem, while in Boston "when a legman called the Hearst city desk with a juicy crime, a rewriteman would ask, 'Is it dark out there?'— meaning is the victim black? If the answer was yes, the reporter was told to forget it." Editors of the *Oakland Tribune* "did not regard a story of a black murdering another black as worth printing." And nonwhites in Houston made the papers only if there were at least three bodies.[13]

In Washington, D.C., which is not only the capital of the United States but the murder capital as well these days, there were 372 murders in 1988. Of these, 351 victims were black, which is to say, 95 percent. Some sociologists and public officials suggest that the young black male is an endangered species.[14] On the other hand, those who defend news media look at such figures and rationalize the policy of not printing stories of black crime because crime is so prevalent among blacks that it has ceased to be newsworthy. This argument may seem plausible, but the fact is that crime is also high among males, people under age 30, and urbanites, and that has not stopped newspapers from printing crime stories about them.

Another defense is that by ignoring crimes involving blacks (as victims or offenders), the media perform a service; printing a glut of stories about crimes involving blacks would exacerbate racial stereotypes and imagery already widespread. This defense might seem reasonable but it is not accurate. Traditionally, the news media have ignored not only black crime but news of every kind about blacks. The long history of blacks being shut out of the news did not come about because sympathetic editors thought neglect was benign. Instead, as the quotes above indicate, deskmen and rewritemen (at the urging of editors) considered blacks and news about them to be of little or no significance.

NONANALYTICAL REPORTING

The rise of objectivity and the inverted-pyramid form made newspapers give less attention to description and stay away from analysis of trends and events.

The telegraph eliminated the correspondent who provided letters that announced an event, described it in detail, and analyzed its substance. It replaced him with the stringer who supplied the bare facts. . . . If the telegraph made prose lean and unadorned and led to a journalism without the luxury of detail and analysis, it also brought an overwhelming crush of such prose to the newsroom.[15]

Those who defend newspapers and belittle television news frequently argue that television presents many stories in such a short span that it serves as little more than a headline service. Newspapers, they say, present in-depth analysis and fill in the outline. While this may be true for some kinds of stories, it does not apply to crime news, where stories containing analysis are highly exceptional. Newspaper norms require crime reporters to accurately report names, ages, dates, locations, and similar details; they do not encourage reporters to wander into more interesting territory by asking questions that go beyond the overt facts of the event itself. Doing more may incur ridicule from colleagues:

On its most basic level . . . there is no theory or supposition required. You collect the facts accurately—who got robbed, who did it, how much was taken, when it happened, and so forth—and you arrange them in a tidy little story of three or four grafs. There is no speculation about real motives, long-term effects on the economy or the political system, or other heavy stuff.[16]

When reporters follow such a know-nothing approach, the crime stories that result are lean on information and practically barren of implication.

Rules of objectivity force reporters to isolate crimes and treat each as a sample of one; they virtually forbid generalizing to the wider picture. Reading about a person mugged in a subway, we do not know whether subways are generally experiencing a rising or declining crime rate. We do not know whether the subway station in question is especially crime-ridden or as safe as others. We do not know whether crowding makes riding subways safer or chancier, whether *this* offense occurs most often or some other crime takes place much more frequently.

If focusing on one crime at a time is the greatest barrier to analysis in crime news, the second greatest is dwelling on the atypical. Actually, the news media penchant for unusual cases surfaces regardless of subject matter, not only in crime. Take divorce, for instance. When asked which social class has the highest divorce rate, my college students usually answer the upper class, and indeed it is true that most divorce cases that make the news involve people of that level. But divorce is far more common in the lower class, where problems and stresses abound, many of them because jobs and money are hard to find or at least hard to keep.

Crime news can be misleading, too, particularly among readers or viewers who are given to generalizing on the basis of one or two cases. Papers in big cities do not cover every crime, not even every murder; there are so many incidents, that they have to be selective. As previously noted, they have certain crimes that they prefer, such as those with an apparently pure and innocent victim and a diabolical offender. But they also like crimes involving persons of prominence (including high social status), be they the victims or the offenders.

Thus, when Joel Steinberg abused his six-year-old "adopted" daughter

Lisa so violently that she died, it was no surprise that this became a cause célèbre in the New York City news media and indeed throughout America, for he was a millionaire lawyer who lived on Fifth Avenue. Unwary readers might have concluded that child abuse is something found commonly in families where the parents are rich, Jewish, or professionally employed. What research we have, however, suggests that none of these conclusions is accurate.

Some reporters said explicitly that child abuse is especially high in recent years and in New York City ("the all-time leader"). To be sure, there has been a spate of articles on child abuse in the news in the past ten years or so. And city bureaucracies that now count child abuse cases or investigations can point to an increase in their figures. But this reflects many other factors in addition to the actual number of children being abused. Agencies are more geared to counting cases than in years past, and citizens are more apt to report abuses than they once were. Indeed, not too many years ago, "child abuse" did not exist as a part of our vocabulary.

Cases did make the news during the 1980s, but this does not mean that the actual incidence of child abuse is higher today than ever before. According to psychohistorian Lloyd DeMause, children throughout the world received harsher treatment the farther back in time we go. Centuries ago, violence and other forms of child abuse were not perceived as social problems at all; in fact, they were widely accepted. In ancient Rome, for example, the law gave fathers the right to do with their children whatever they wished and explicitly included the right to sell, sacrifice, mutilate or kill them.[17]

Inherent in the criticism of the nonanalytical nature of newspapers is the belief that news accounts of crime should be much more interpretive than they are. This might seem to be asking a lot, but the fact is that some papers do supply analyses; examples include the *New York Times*, *Washington Post*, and *San Jose Mercury*, all of which have telephoned me for comment on some criminological question or another. If they have called me, surely they have prevailed on more famous criminologists. The *New York Times* quoted one expert, who provided some interesting insights on the Steinberg case.

"Often the battering man is not abusive to the kids, especially when they're young. But as they grow older, that can sometimes change." Larry Weinberg . . . believed this pattern fits the relationship he knew. Mr. Steinberg, who is a lawyer, saw Elizabeth "as a compliant partner or ally against Hedda" [the woman Steinberg battered often and badly], Mr. Weinberg said.

He said that he believed that Elizabeth became old enough "to try to intervene and defend Hedda, and suddenly bore the brunt" of Mr. Steinberg's rage.[18]

FRAGMENTING

Fragments are unrelated stories that make news difficult for readers to remember and put into some larger context. "Making connections between events is disallowed by the journalistic format, for the news media's unit of analysis is the news item: a self-contained particle of 'reality.' "[19] This is what Barbara Phillips calls the mosaic effect. Furthermore, each day news people wipe the slate clean, for daily news means the birth of new information and the destruction of all that is old. Newspapers, in effect, shield readers from history, seldom referring to the past, even that of just a few months ago. They normally do not fill in the links between events and fail to show how these combine to form a coherent pattern.

In a chaotic universe, with people hurtling in a meaningless void, there would be no reason for newspapers to search for connections, but it is a rare human being who sees only chaos and wants this vision reinforced by the news media. Most people believe that order and predictability govern their daily lives and the broader world as well. They count on observers of this broader world to discover these elements of predictability and relay them to their audiences.

If the media do tell readers and viewers about anyone in great detail, it is the American president. They follow him everywhere he goes, reporting on him, his advisers, his family, even the First Pet. We are told which president ate cottage cheese and ketchup for lunch, and which one likes pork rinds. When newspapers say that they provide the whole story, not just the headlines, this is most true of their coverage of the president.

Yet even presidential news coverage tends toward the fragmentary, as reporters tend to assemble a few shards of information daily from speeches, press releases, and interviews that sources within the administration provide. As a rule, these sources have institutional interests and obligations to protect, not to mention careers, so many of them cannot afford to reveal all that they know, especially if what they know reflects badly on the president or the cabinet department. While the rise of a prying investigative press has been noted often, most modern presidents have been spared: details of their murky pasts typically fail to reach print until after they have retired or died. Even then, the information appears in biographies rather than newspapers.

Richard Nixon and Lyndon Johnson reached the Oval Office without the American public knowing much about them, although both had long careers in the Washington spotlight: in the House of Representatives, the Senate, and later the vice-presidency. They had to be visible over the years, cultivating voters and favorable publicity. But journalists made only feeble attempts to uncover the salient details of their pasts. Reasonably complete and revealing descriptions did not appear until after their demises, when the need for such details was of course less pressing.

Johnson's early life in Texas was little known to Americans, because reporters and researchers did not probe it extensively, that is, not until Robert Caro's biography of Johnson after his death. Caro's findings came as a shock to nearly all who read his work, in fact, to Caro, too, who had not anticipated finding Johnson to be so unscrupulous and scheming. Previously, the lore available on the early life of Johnson had come mostly from Johnson himself, certainly a voluble source but not, it seems, a reliable one.

Nixon's years in California and in the House of Representatives were likewise shrouded in some mystery. Again, the misinformation was aided by researchers' failing to investigate him very diligently and by Nixon supplying his own gloss or interpretation. He liked to reminisce some of the time, but he also provided more permanent pieces of information in his books such as *Six Crises* (and in his nationally televised Checkers Speech).

The latter appeal in 1952 urged Americans to keep him on the Eisenhower ticket after a few newspapers had accused Nixon of maintaining a slush fund. In defending the fund, Nixon said that he needed the money because he was poor, that the money was used for political rather than personal needs, and that he did nothing in return for the California businessmen who had given him the $18,000 or so. Newspapers never questioned Nixon on these claims or checked into whether his benefactors reaped anything for their dollars. In fact, these businessmen did receive favors from Nixon, so many that there is not room here for the details, and they were not reported in 1952, when a summary article would have been most appropriate. Instead, Americans had to wait 37 years before the information finally surfaced, and then as part of a biography, not in the news media.[20] Because the stories behind the Checkers Speech went uninvestigated, Nixon wiggled out of trouble and into the public's good graces.

In more recent years, the press has shown a similar reluctance to confront the Reagan administration. What is conventionally termed an adversarial relationship gave way to something more like cooptation, as television news people allowed the White House almost to set the agenda: what pictures would be taken and what would be the issues of the day. Congressional Democrats, believing Reagan too powerful to risk challenging, abdicated their role as the opposition, leaving the phalanx of White House public-relations specialists to dominate the discussion. This pulled political debate further to the right during the 1980s. When serious problems did crop up for the administration, the press seemed unprepared and unsure of what questions to ask. Reagan did not emerge completely unscathed from the scandal, but he faced milder probing than other presidents would have encountered.

The same soft press could be found in city government. In New York City, for example, the major news outlets are world famous, but they failed to pin down the mayor, Ed Koch, on the crime and corruption so prominent in his administration. Initially, he had run as a reformer, promising to hire people based solely on their merit and fitness, not on cronyism. But upon entering the campaign, reality set in, and he decided that winning the election would require that he strike a deal with the political bosses of Brooklyn, Queens, and the Bronx. If they would agree to support his candidacy and get out the vote in their boroughs, he would reciprocate by hiring some of their favorites once he took over city hall. They agreed to the arrangement, and when Koch won, the stream of tainted newcomers came with him, though his own personnel panels had deemed them manifestly unqualified.

After a few years of such hiring, a fairly sizable number of officials of dubious backgrounds were ensconced in city government. Eventually, some of them were caught, and one by one they left office in disgrace, some landing in prison. After each scandal, the mayor would ask reporters if they thought he personally was in any way corrupt. We might expect the press to take this as a challenge and begin investigating his ties to the borough bosses but it did not. Reporters allowed Koch's excuses and off-the-cuff responses to each new exposure to stand undisputed. Reporters showed no interest in discovering what could be behind the facade of the reformer.

CONCLUSION

In ordinary parlance, bias refers to ideological leaning as opposed to objectivity. In sociology, however, it means something much broader, namely, systematic (nonrandom) measurement error, which can be found almost anywhere, including in the media. Whenever reporters have to compress a multifarious reality into a few paragraphs, distortion inevitably results, particularly when some parts are deliberately highlighted and others completely left out, which happens in every news story written. Therefore, in the sociological sense, communication biases are ever present.

In the olden days, crime reporting biases were most evident in the press's fascination with blood and gore; Hearstian crimes, a favorite of yellow journalism, appeared regularly in many newspapers around the turn of the century. Most newspapers of today do not stoop that low, but exceptions can be found, among them the *New York Post* headline of a few years back: HEADLESS BODY IN TOPLESS BAR.

Few will agree with me, but I believe that in newspapers of today the most common bias is the pulling of punches. In political reporting, journalists will occasionally touch on crime and corruption items but rarely do they plunge into these stories very thoroughly. In New York City, for instance, political corruption has such a notorious history that schoolchildren for years have been taught about the Tweed Gang and its machinations. It is now part of our cultural lore. But in the 1980s, the *New York Times*, considered the world's greatest and most influential paper, did not address city government very much and did not acknowledge the slide toward municipal corruption until too late. The *Village Voice* did, but few people took that paper seriously; not many even read it. The *Times*, preferring to be upbeat, ignored the city and its problems. When it did finally cover the scandal, the damage had already been done.

By the 1980s the *Times* had essentially stopped covering city government. [Veteran reporters were replaced by youngsters, who] spent inordinate time searching out the soft features that filled the metropolitan section. Hard news suffered. In terms of City Hall coverage, the *Times* skipped along the visible peaks [of ceremonial appearances while ignoring] who received contracts, and why, and how they performed.[21]

The scandal in New York City was not well covered, nor was coverage of the Reagan administration's scandal a source of pride for the press. Again, the press pulled punches by going soft and trusting the highest authorities, who seemed likable and honest.

Americans were told not about a president who harbored an apparently pathological disregard for truth, but about a well-meaning Everyman who at times got his figures wrong. As presidential scholar James David Barber observed: "Ronald Reagan is the first modern president whose contempt for the facts is treated as a charming idiosyncrasy."[22]

The *New York Times* was not alone, but it led this movement toward softness, in part, because the publisher stepped in and warned his editor that crusading investigative journalism was going too far—it was alienating corporate advertisers.

Crime of a nonpolitical nature also lack a hard edge in news reports, as news people find gratification in small details and rudimentary facts, such as ages, names, dates, times, and addresses, but pay scant attention to relationships between victim and offender or the cultural setting of the crime. Cautioned against any signs of critical thinking, crime reporters hug the shoreline, relying heavily on perfunctory findings by police and treating each crime in splendid isolation.

Crimes surface with great regularity, and some of them spark our interest, but merely to point to them as novelties is insufficient. They are a recurring phenomenon, and they have some important commonalities that only a superficial approach would overlook. Yet crime reporters overlook them as a rule. They do not do the kind of probing we would expect from a college sophomore. They do not even ask why the United States in general, and cities in particular, have so much crime.

In its cautious approach of raising small questions and sticking to the case at hand, the press appears as a paper tiger. Articles often dwell on the narrowest of particulars, leaving crime in general alone. The omission of broader discussions rarely startles readers, who have been conditioned not to expect them. After years of such narrowness, it has become sanctified by journalistic custom.

NOTES

1. James Ford, *Forty-Odd Years in the Literary Shop* (New York: Dutton, 1921), p. 260.

2. Suzanne Daley, "Man Tells Police He Shot Youths on Subway Train," *New York Times*, January 1, 1985, p. 1.

3. "Man Admits Shooting 4 on Subway," *Atlanta Journal-Constitution*, January 1, 1985, p. 1.

4. "Subway Vigilante Gives Himself Up," *New York Post*, January 1, 1985, p. 1.

5. Edna Buchanan, *The Corpse Had a Familiar Face* (New York: Random House, 1987), p. 6.

6. Timothy Crouse, *The Boys on the Bus* (New York: Ballantine, 1973), pp. 280–281.

7. James Neal and Suzanne Brown, *Newswriting and Reporting* (Ames: Iowa State University Press, 1976), p. 101.

8. Bob Schieffer and Gary Paul Gates, *The Acting President* (New York: Dutton, 1989), p. 12.

9. John Chancellor and Walter Mears, *The News Business* (New York: Harper and Row, 1983), p. 111.

10. William Burrows, *On Reporting the News* (New York: New York University Press, 1977), p. 184.

11. David Pritchard, "Race, Homicide and Newspapers," *Journalism Quarterly* 62 (Autumn 1985): 500.

12. Russell Baker, *Good Times* (New York: Morrow, 1989), p. 77.

13. J. Anthony Lukas, *Common Ground* (New York: Knopf, 1985); A. M. Rosenthal, *Thirty-Eight Witnesses* (New York: McGraw-Hill, 1964); Rodney Stark, *Sociology* (Belmont, CA: Wadsworth, 1989); Linda Ellerbee, *And So It Goes* (New York: Putnam, 1986).

14. Bill McAllister, "The Menaced Lives of Black Men," *New York Newsday*, January 3, 1990, p. 15.

15. James Carey, "The Dark Continent of American Journalism," in *Reading*

the News, ed. Robert Manoff and Michael Schudson (New York: Pantheon, 1987), p. 165.

16. Burrows, *On Reporting the News*, p. 181.

17. Roger Bybee, "Violence Toward Youth," *Journal of Social Issues* 35 (Spring 1979): 1–14; Lloyd DeMause, *The History of Childhood* (New York: Psychohistory Press, 1974).

18. Steven Erlanger, "A Widening Pattern of Abuse Exemplified in Steinberg Case," *New York Times*, November 8, 1987, pp. 2, 44.

19. Barbara Phillips, "Novelty Without Change," *Journal of Communication* 26 (Autumn 1976): 89.

20. Roger Morris, *Richard Milhous Nixon* (New York: Henry Holt, 1990), p. 821.

21. Joseph Goulden, *Fit to Print* (Secaucus, NJ: Lyle Stuart, 1988), p. 248.

22. Mark Hertsgaard, *On Bended Knee* (New York: Farrar, Straus and Giroux, 1988), p. 138.

Chapter Five

Deviance in the News

Conservatives feel aggrieved. They believe the American press has undermined their causes and embraced those of the liberal-left. Ironically, this accusation comes at a time when Republicans have taken up nearly permanent residence in the White House by winning five of the six presidential campaigns between 1968 and 1988. While Republicans were winning those five, Democrats were mustering only 14 percent of the electoral college. Mondale and McGovern each won 1 state out of 50, showings more futile than some third-party candidates have made over the years (John Bell, Teddy Roosevelt, Strom Thurmond and George Wallace).

NEWS AND NIXON

What kind of reasoning could prompt conservative thinkers, when their party is flushed with success, to denounce the press for luring the general public to the left? In search of an answer, we could start with the early experiences of Richard Nixon as filtered through his perceptual lens. From the beginning of his life in politics, he considered the press to be united in opposing him and character assassins intent upon smearing him. He said he was accused of "bigamy, forgery, drunkenness, insanity, thievery, anti-Semitism, perjury—the whole gamut of misconduct in public affairs."[1] We have no way of knowing whether such accusations were made early in his career, since Nixon does not present any supporting evidence. We have only his word to go by.

When he lost the presidential race in 1960, Nixon blamed Kennedy sympathizers in the press. Two years later, bristling with anger after failing in his campaign to become governor of California, the man of somber mien said, "As I leave you I want you to know—just think how much you're going to be missing. You won't have Nixon to kick around any more."[2] But he changed his mind, and when he returned he won the presidency. In a special 1969 television address he appealed to the silent majority to support the war in Vietnam. Dismayed by television's instant analysis, he told Pat Buchanan to draft some blistering speeches that would strike fear in the tormenting media, speeches that Spiro Agnew would deliver.

Though Nixon complained about the press, few political figures received better treatment than he. Instead of scrutinizing his record, newspapers led the early campaigns for him. As David Halberstam has pointed out, their headlines repeated his charges against opponents.[3] In his first campaign, Nixon had "70 percent more advertising than the incumbent, more than two and one-half times the news stories, some thirty-eight favorable editorials to two for the incumbent." And *LA Times* endorsements of Nixon were taped inside the voting booths.[4] While running for the Senate in 1950, he won editorial support and "almost exclusive coverage of more than 240 [out of 250] California newspapers in which criticism of any stripe was virtually unknown, and the blackout of [his opponent] Helen Douglas . . . all but complete."[5]

Once the Pentagon Papers were released, Nixon, then president, grew more audacious. He hounded reporters with IRS audits, phone taps, and other irritants. In his thinking, the eastern media were the entrenched enemy, not amenable to persuasion by conservatives. They would continue to wield power, manage and manipulate the news, giving it a liberal slant.[6] Anyone harboring doubts about these matters of faith knew it wise to keep quiet; those who did not would soon find themselves left out of the White House's cherished inner circle.

Edith Efron did not question these beliefs, but she did seek confirmation and claimed to have found it in television news coverage of events in 1968. She said that television news then showed a definite bias against the middle class, the Johnson war policy, and especially against Richard Nixon.[7] After Efron's book *The News Twisters* came out, other conservatives joined the bandwagon. Accuracy in Media founder Reed Irvine pestered targets with frequent letters and columns. (Not all targets took his barbs with grace. Ben Bradlee, for instance, fired back, calling Irvine "a miserable, carping, retromingent [that is, backward-urinating] vigilante."[8]) Instead of stray potshots, Kevin Phillips presented a thoughtful, comprehensive analysis, arguing that the media were largely conservative in the 1950s and remained so in the South, Midwest, and Rockies. Later, however, they acquired power as great as the nineteenth-century trusts and monopolies once enjoyed. With such power, and ensconced in liberal surroundings, media people began embracing liberal causes (against war, poverty, and hunger).[9]

The assault of conservatives on the media culminated in *The Media Elite*, a study by Lichter, Rothman, and Lichter of employees at the *New York Times, Washington Post, Wall Street Journal, Time, Newsweek, U.S. News and World Report*, and the television networks.[10] It claimed that news people form a homogeneous white male elite who (1) were raised in the large cities of the northeast by upper-middle-class parents and (2) hold leftist views on social issues. Earlier, Nixon expressed the same idea: "the *New York Times, Washington Post, Time, Newsweek* and the three television networks, you will find overwhelmingly that their editorial bias comes down on the side of amnesty, pot and abortion."[11] This hypothesis can be tested by determining what elite newspapers say about deviance and social problems.

DEVIANCE AND SOCIAL PROBLEMS

Deviance usually includes drug use or abuse, alcoholism, mental illness, suicide, prostitution, crime, and delinquency. But some sociologists find this list too long (labeling theorists, in particular), while others think it too short. Russell Baker is a columnist rather than sociologist, but he has suggested that it is also considered deviant to tell ethnic jokes, appear overweight in public, smoke in taxis and restaurants, or act like a male chauvinist.[12] While examining deviance in the news, the traditional list will be kept in mind here but it will not be treated as gospel.

To determine what it means to lean left on these issues, we must consult deviance theories. Howard Becker's labeling or interactionist theory stands as the most obvious example of a liberal perspective. He maintains that whether an activity is considered deviant depends on how other people react to it—not on the nature of the act itself. Therefore behavior is itself neither deviant nor conventional. Rules tend not to be enforced very consistently, and this allows enforcers to make the poor and powerless bear the brunt.

Becker says that getting apprehended gives people a new status, such as lunatic, whore, or juvenile delinquent. Once labeled, people are presumed to engage in deviant behavior again and again; thus these are the people that police first turn to when a similar act is committed later on. Stigma gets generalized, too, so that those who are accused of one kind of deviance are expected to commit other deviant acts as well (lying, cheating, and stealing, for example).

Deviance, according to Becker, is a master status. Regardless of a person's other qualities, labels such as delinquent or alcoholic carry the greatest weight when others evaluate him or her. A self-fulfilling prophecy may also arise. The labeled person may not be deeply involved in deviance, but the label forces him or her to sever ties with conventional groups and turn to deviance to make a living. Therefore, deviance actually results from the hostile reactions of others.

Becker devotes special attention to people he calls moral entrepreneurs—crusaders who set their sights on an activity they regard as especially repugnant, then expose it to public attention. They tend to categorize behavior as good or bad and ask that the latter be stamped out by any available means. Moral entrepreneurs have directed their wrath at alcohol, gambling, prostitution, homosexuality, and other behaviors and commodities. Often they view their mission as a holy one.

When legislation is passed, moral crusaders recede into the background, and law enforcers assume a central role. Unlike moral entrepreneurs, though, police know from experience that the "evil" will not be eradicated, so they give up trying to enforce special laws. Instead, they focus on how deviants respond to them. The offender who displays a sullen attitude toward police may be arrested, while more cooperative individuals are released; police enjoy great latitude and discretion in deciding whom to arrest—more evidence, according to Becker, that deviance is not inherent in a given behavior but results from the application of negative sanctions.[13]

Finally, labeling theorists adopt a tolerant attitude toward deviants, viewing them as essentially benign. Hence, they advocate that society permit "the widest possible diversity of behaviors and attitudes" rather than forcing people to adjust to the narrow and arbitrary standards of the general society.[14] The laissez-faire philosophy entails leaving deviants alone and letting them be deviant without ever calling them that.

A more radical theory differs from the labeling theory in several respects. Radicals object to the labeling theorists' style, which is to mingle with deviant groups and describe how these people, society's innocent underdogs, are treated unfairly by low-level officials such as police or mental hospital workers. Radical theorists say that this blames the individual instead of the system and is thus short-sighted. (Conservatives also blame persons instead of the system, but in this case the individuals blamed are the deviants rather than the low-level officials.) If radical theorists had their way, theories would concentrate on large-scale social, political, and economic forces. According to radical thinking, the spread of deviant behavior goes hand in glove with the vastly unequal distribution of power and wealth in America.

Radicals believe that capitalism puts pressure on companies to increase productivity and reduce labor costs, objectives often achieved by laying off people from work. This makes some individuals superfluous to the economy, so they may turn to the underground economy or some comparably disreputable improvisation. Living on the margin of society makes them susceptible to other forms of deviance (alcoholism, drugs, child abuse, and spouse abuse) as they become more disenchanted and frustrated.

At the other end of the spectrum, the power elite may also engage in deviance. Corporations, according to the radicals, may rob through tax breaks, price fixing, bribery, and selling shoddy merchandise. They prevail on friends in the media not to expose these practices and undermine consumer confidence and on congressional friends not to pass bills inimical to company interests. Most corporate violations and schemes do not come to light, and those that do rarely bring swift retribution, because regulatory agencies may be weak, understaffed, or coopted by the industry. Radicals believe that more intellectuals should make it their business to penetrate the corporate hierarchy and expose the crime and corruption it shields.

FALL OF THE MIGHTY

For six weeks in July and August of 1987, I consulted three papers— the *Chicago Tribune*, *Philadelphia Inquirer*, and *Washington Post*—each one honored and esteemed in the world of journalism today and thus qualifying as elite media (the focus of the Nixon and Lichter et al. arguments). During this period, several White House figures landed on the front pages and in hot water soon after leaving the administration for the private sector to become highly paid lobbyists. Stories about Lyn Nofziger were hard news items: Nofziger indicted, pleads not guilty, and the like, but those about Michael Deaver were more engaging. The *Washington Post* said that three kinds of people would discuss him:

The first are real friends who love and admire him. . . . The next . . . have clashed with Deaver and today will tell a wicked story or two. But they are loath to pour too much salt on the wounds. . . . In the third group are people who . . . are damned if they'll let you leave with the impression that his day in the sun didn't change him.[15]

One former Reagan official said that Deaver flouted one of Washington's most fundamental, though unstated, rules: Don't brag about being a power broker. He said that Deaver never realized such a rule existed, perhaps because he lived nearly all his life in California, where "if you got your picture on the cover of *Time* magazine riding around in a limousine [which Deaver did], that would be good news."[16] This idea, that what is deviant in Washington, D.C., is perfectly normal in California, is in keeping with labeling theory. As we shall see, however, other stories were not.

White House staffers were not the only officials to fall from grace. Bess Myerson, a one-time Miss America, began her descent when she hired a young woman to work for her in the New York City Commission of Cultural Affairs. At the time, the aging Myerson was being courted by millionaire sewer contractor Andy Capasso, who was serving time in prison for tax evasion and who was also trying to reduce his financial obligations to his ex-wife. The judge in the financial case was Hortense Gabel, who just happened to be the mother of Sukhreet Gabel, who just happened to be the woman Myerson went out of her way to hire and befriend. After Sukhreet Gabel began working for Myerson, Hortense Gabel started slashing Capasso's payments to his ex-wife. This was either a tit-for-tat arrangement or a believe-it-or-not coincidence; thinking it the former, prosecutors put Myerson, Capasso, and Judge Gabel on trial.

Misdeeds of police, landlords, and doctors also made the news. In Mexico City, for instance, police bribed, bullied, robbed, and assaulted ordinary people in the street, while in Philadelphia an officer illegally arrested, handcuffed, and beat an Asian man because neighbors disliked having Asians live in their midst. Farther west:

In Los Angeles, a landlord began serving a 30-day sentence . . . amid the rat droppings, cockroaches, broken glass and falling plaster of a tenement he has repeatedly refused to repair.

Beverly Hills neurosurgeon Milton Avol was fitted with an "electronic leash" . . . to keep him near the building until repairs are made. The judge . . . "wants to make sure that he stays where he is."[17]

In showing society's poor and powerless being abused by the powerful, these articles are radical. But most of the abusers acted alone, not as representatives of the power elite, so the stories are not so radical after all. They do follow the labeling tradition when they provide an inside look at deviants, particularly when they describe these people as genial and endearing. But by extending this sympathy to people near the seats of power (Myerson and Deaver) instead of to the underclass, these stories do not fit the labeling tradition.

RACE

Radical theory calls racism, sexism, poverty, and imperialism the real crimes. Though a few articles mentioned racism, these were about incidents from the past. On July 8, 1987, the *Chicago Tribune* carried an item on the first black officers to enter the navy (back in the 1940s). Reminiscing about those days, the men said that when they entered an officers club for the first time, the white officers there immediately stalked out. Another story, in the *Washington Post* on July 7, 1987, profiled Larry Doby, the first black to play baseball in the American League. Doby, reflecting on his rookie year, said that when he was introduced to his Cleveland Indian teammates, they refused to shake hands. Opposing players and managers, such as Casey Stengel were worse, hectoring him constantly with epithets such as "coon" and "jigaboo." Doby, unlike Jackie Robinson, had an ego too frail for such abuse.[18] Though they sympathize with blacks, these stories do not constitute radical statements, because (1) they are not general analyses and (2) they hinge on events long past, leaving the implication that racism has since withered away—an idea not at all radical.

Another story covered a more recent development. The mayor of Portsmouth, Virginia, a black man, had been thought of as his city's savior. He had helped rescue it when it had fallen on hard times; but he later found himself in trouble, because of some excessive expenditures while in office and some threatening letters sent to local community leaders. These letters were traced through fingerprinting back to the mayor.[19] Had the letters been the work of some disgruntled whites, the article might have had a liberal or radical message. But hate mail from a fellow black leader turns this into a very different kind of story.

WOMEN

The *Chicago Tribune, Philadelphia Inquirer*, and *Washington Post* sometimes write about women as victims—of bias, harassment, or attack. In one of these stories, a doctor used anesthesia to put patients under, then photographed them nude or sexually assaulted them. Officials might never have learned of these incidents if it were not for his wife, who occasionally worked in his office (and who later divorced him). She found the pictures and turned them over to the police, but they were not accustomed to arresting medical doctors and wished nothing to do with the case. The wife therefore retrieved the evidence and took it to the state's attorney, who agreed to prosecute.[20]

Another article discussed sexual harassment at work. Ordinarily this kind of case involves a woman complaining that a man in the office made an overt pass at her. In this case, however, the woman said that the entire office (the Washington regional office of the Securities and Exchange Commission) was permeated with an atmosphere of sexual harassment: drunkenness at office parties, affairs between managers and underlings, promotions and awards given employees involved with their manager, and promotions denied whoever complained of the goings-on. This was the complainant's side of the story; at the end of the article, the reporter gave the rebuttal—officials called her an unsatisfactory worker with a personality disorder.[21]

The story about bias took place in Philadelphia, where a young woman became the first female assigned to the police department's prestigious homicide unit. She said she was being frozen out of mundane activities simply because of her sex. Initially when she joined the unit, things ran smoothly, and she built a reputation for solving celebrated murders. But when a new captain took over, he made her drop all active investigations and even forbade her to transport male prisoners. She took her grievance through police channels but to no avail. Soon she was expelled from the unit. She mulled things over, then reluctantly decided to sue.[22]

The stories about blacks and women do not staunchly support labeling theory, for they portray racism and sexism as breaches of conduct that fully warrant punishment. Labeling theory, in contrast, indulges offenders and regards nothing as inherently deviant. According to it, each social group has its standards and should not presume to impose them on anyone else. Fervently embracing cultural relativism, labeling theory encourages people to appreciate deviants and their viewpoint, which, naturally, is that what they do is perfectly normal.

Discerning readers will detect in labeling theory a protest or backlash against the 1950s, when affluent whites moved to the suburbs in record number, purchased cars and backyard barbecues, and joined churches. Television programs such as *Father Knows Best* now seem hopelessly unrealistic to us but were fairly authentic in some ways at the time. Certainly, family life was thriving. Marriages were on the rise and divorces receding. Pronatalism burst forth in full flower after 200 years of declining birth rates.

Anti-communism helped push America toward a more homogenized culture, where pressures were to get along. Some parents cared more about their child's popularity than his or her report card. Some of America's premier sociologists took note of these developments. David Riesman, for instance, warned about the new other-directedness; William H. Whyte dissected the organization man; and Daniel Bell announced the end of ideology.[23] During the 1950s, there was not much talk of abortion, the drug culture was small and hidden, and homosexuals remained in the closet.

Labeling theorists surveying this scene saw that deviance was neither extensive nor threatening; it merely ran afoul of the Protestant ethic, which never held them in thrall anyway—they much preferred the hang-loose ethic. So they become *advocates* of deviance. Then things changed. Following the upheavals and social movements of the 1960s, the field of deviance expanded to include racism, sexism, child abuse, and spouse abuse. If labeling theory was to remain faithful to its doctrine, it could only argue that these behaviors were not truly deviant and people engaging in them deserved neither stigma nor punishment.

HUSBAND/WIFE STORIES

Several stories let readers spy on marriages in the process of falling to pieces. Crumbling marriages are far from rare, so to merit space in the newspaper they must be accompanied by more than the hurling of pottery and epithets. Something serious is required—murder or bludgeoning. The story of Mary Baker contained such ingredients. Her husband kept her a virtual

prisoner in her apartment. She said he refused to allow her to receive telephone calls but insisted she take messages from his girlfriends. He told her [she should] walk only between their front and back doors. She said he . . . slapped her so hard that her glasses flew off and threatened [to] cut their unborn baby out of her stomach.[24]

One day, without warning, she retaliated by throwing a pot of boiling water on him and shooting him twice, leaving him blind in one eye and burned over 25 percent of his body. She was sentenced to prison.

The Baker story was news only in Chicago, but the marital distress of Joan Collins and Peter Holm made headlines in newspapers and magazines across the world, because of her fame on the show *Dynasty*. A *Washington Post* reporter decided their story could be treated with levity:

Joan Collins, in case you have been in a hole for a while, is trying to get a divorce. It is expensive to get a divorce if you live in Los Angeles and make $95,000 an episode. Usually it is expensive for men, who are frequently to be found shedding their wives and former popsies here at very great cost and some embarrassment . . . but we are in a new era now, and thus these vistas have been opened to women also.[25]

Holm's former girlfriend testified that he once told her to marry a wealthy octogenarian while he (Holm) would marry and defraud Collins; then, when they were free of these spouses, they could marry each other and share their newfound wealth.

In another article, John, who in 1969 ended his tour in Vietnam as a helicopter pilot, returned home and married his long-time sweetheart. He believed that his was a happy and satisfying marriage; but his wife thought otherwise. After 18 years of married life,

John thought he had all the amenities of a happy home: nice cars, house in the suburbs, three kids and a loving wife. He knew his nuptial bliss would last forever. Unfortunately, forever came last March . . . when he confronted his wife with his suspicions of her being involved in an extramarital affair. To his as-

80 CRIME AND THE AMERICAN PRESS

tonishment and dismay, she didn't deny the claim. Rather than have her walk
out of his life for good, they agreed that she would spend equal time with both
men.[26]

This must be a new form of time sharing.

Finally, one couple had problems so fundamental that their marriage
ended without having begun. Edward gave Peggy an engagement ring,
and they agreed to get married on April 10; on April 8, Peggy's parents
generously sold him their house for far below its market value. Half an
hour later, Edward told Peggy that he did not love her, had never found
her attractive, and did not plan to marry her. What he did plan was to
sell the house at a great profit and file suit, demanding that she return
his ring.[27]

While not pro-wife in every detail, these stories seem to side with the
women in most confrontations. The men described herein do not appear
charming. Except for the helicopter pilot, they are greedy, inept, or
uncouth. And the sympathy extended to the pilot may be due in part
to his apparent lack of machismo (he has crying bouts and participates
in psychotherapy).

Is there a radical slant to these portraits? If there is such a thing as a
radical analysis of marital conflict, it would trace the problems to our
capitalist economy, which has traditionally hired men for outside work
and treated housework as superfluous. Husbands try to control both
the family finances and the sexual relationship. When employers make
working conditions exploitive, men/workers/husbands vent their frustrations on the most convenient target, their wives. Newspapers do not
pursue this line of argument. Radical analyses of the family are unthink-
able, because (1) newspapers do not probe family matters in any depth
and (2) conservative readers would not stand for them.

CHILD ABUSE

Stories of failed marriages can be disheartening, but they do not often
shock us; some may even be amusing. But humor never enters stories
of child abuse, where the tone is somber. In two stories, mothers were
charged with killing their babies by starvation. A three-month-old
weighed six pounds at death, which was less than he weighed at birth.
The other, similarly underfed, had sores, sunken eyes, and dirt in every
crevice.[28]

Serious as these cases are, others were worse. In one story, a six-year-
old girl was talking to a man who, after learning that her father was
asleep and her mother away, returned with two others to burglarize the
apartment. Seeing them brazenly go about their business, the girl complained, whereupon one of them "started to strangle her and bashed

her head on the floor, knocking her out. While the other accomplices carried out the goods, [he] allegedly raped the girl. The girl has not regained consciousness."[29] In another case, three men raped a 14-year-old girl, tied her behind a car, and dragged her through the Chicago streets. She required skin grafts to patch her face together and hospitalization to get over the emotional trauma. The treatment failed, for she still lashes out, though the objects of her rages are innocent parties.[30]

Finally, the *Chicago Tribune* profiled a doctor whose job is to treat abused children who are admitted to Cook County Hospital. She has seen the results of persecution ranging from the offensive to the unspeakable; that so little has been done by officials to help the victims troubles her greatly. Almost as much as the abuses themselves. All of us have heard of children being dipped into a pot of boiling water or burned with cigarettes or whipped and punched. This article delved into several other, more exotic abuses that occur: some parents shake their babies so violently that they become brain-damaged, and some have strapped their babies to a toilet for six months. Other incidents dwell on depravities that do not bear repeating.[31]

Mistreatment of frail, defenseless children offends most reporters, as these articles reveal. But can we confidently paint them as belonging to one political camp—liberal, radical, or conservative? If liberal means conforming to labeling theory, then they are not liberal, for they do not say that child abuse is benign and abusers should be spared punishment. They are not radical either, for they do not claim that grinding poverty caused by the inequities of capitalism makes parents become abusive. Nor are the articles very conservative. Many conservatives believe that the family is the main institution holding society together; without strong family discipline, children will grow up wild, unsocialized, and disruptive. In short, conservatives insist that families should stay intact and parents should exert firm control. When that control spills over into outright abuse, conservatives do not become very upset about it.

AIDS

At one time, articles addressing the topic of AIDS focused almost exclusively on the link between it and homosexuality. After driving that connection into the ground, news media began to consider AIDS and the IV drug user. In a *Chicago Tribune* article, the reporter began with the death of Tito, who succumbed after ten years of using drugs. When an ex-addict was asked what effect this death would have on other junkies from the same block as Tito, he said it would not deter them at all: "They don't care 'bout nothing but shooting up. They are starting to hear about AIDS on the street now, but they ain't changing."[32] What makes them refuse to change, said the ex-addict, is their fatalism. Although others on the same corner had recently died of AIDS, "what does that mean out here when the presumption is you are going to die young anyway of either a bullet or an overdose? What does the added threat of dying of AIDS mean? These people are addicts. They've already put the gun to their head. Addicts are suicidal. AIDS to them is just another way to die."[33]

Another article suggested that education could stem the spread of AIDS from addicts to the general public. While Chicago addicts were on the increase, the city was doing little to educate them about AIDS. City officials balked at the idea of funding anyone as marginal as drug users, and addicts (who generally mistrusted city officials) were loath to seek help on their own initiative. Even if addicts and city officials had seen eye-to-eye, it is not likely that local residents would have allowed rehab centers to be built in their backyards.

Other stories on the illness dealt with the personal threat: a male prostitute selling AIDS-tainted blood to a plasma center and a prisoner with AIDS urinating on guards who tried moving him to a different cell. Most interesting was a *Washington Post* story that began this way:

John Bwalya was supposed to sleep last fall with Alice, his brother's widow. The Zambians call it "cleansing." When a man dies, his widow is expected to have sex with one of her inlaws, usually a brother. According to a widely held traditional belief, this rids her of the ghost of her husband and frees her to remarry.

Bwalya says he was afraid to sleep with Alice, because his brother, after a year's illness, had died of . . . AIDS. Despite pressures from the widow, her family and his own uncle, Bwalya adamantly refused to cleanse his sister-in-law. With the help of a sympathetic older brother, [he] fled his home village. "It was like someone bringing you a coffin and saying you get in . . . ," says Bwalya. The AIDS epidemic that has swept across Africa in the past five years has been exacerbated in Zambia by deeply entrenched tribal customs.[34]

Bubbling just below the surface of these articles, and indeed most discussions of AIDS, are two ideas: that addicts are expendable, and we will get serious about AIDS when it begins posing a greater threat to nonaddicts and nonhomosexuals. AIDS might seem to be the perfect subject to which news people could apply the labeling perspective, but they did not avail themselves of the opportunity.

HOMOSEXUALITY

Stories dealing with homosexuality focused on denials. One article by a historian said that J. Edgar Hoover sent agents to track down rumors that he was a homosexual and to tell the sources that he was not and that they had better shut up.[35] Jim Bakker and others also denied the rumors but had no agents to call upon. Two people said that they were: San Francisco writer Armistead Maupin and Congressman Barney Frank. Frank had long assumed that being homosexual ruled out running for political office. After running and winning, however, he decided to keep his private life a secret, but a former congressman who was gay wrote a book in which he revealed Frank's homosexuality. This and several other developments finally spurred Frank into disclosing his sexual orientation.

The feature articles on Maupin and Frank were openly sympathetic, while the spot news item on Jim Bakker was not. Several explanations for this difference seem plausible. First, reporters appreciate long interviews, especially those replete with candid discussions of uncomfortable secrets in one's personal life. They consider "no comment" less kindly, more of a slap in the face. Second, they pounce on hypocrisy by smug, sanctimonious individuals trying to hide something shadowy. Third, reporters are especially critical of a person who seduces someone then threatens to fire him if he talks, which may have been the case with Bakker.[36]

If there is a radical position on homosexuality, I do not know what it is. I can speculate on these matters but, to paraphrase Herbert Marcuse, not every problem that someone has with his sex life is necessarily due to the capitalist mode of production. (Of course, there are many individuals who believe homosexuality is not a problem.) The three papers in this sample seem to waver between left and right. They are conservative when making accusations but liberal when admiring a person for coming out of the closet.

DRUGS

Drug selling is one of the most remunerative of all businesses in the higher echelons. On the other hand, it is one of the riskiest for pushers, who have been known to get arrested, robbed, beaten, or killed when deals go sour. Users are also sometimes victims, due to overdose, disease, addiction, arrest, and so on. This theme, that top dogs prosper while underlings run the risks, is one that papers do not emphasize. Instead, they seem to stress that people in the drug trade are alien invaders. Not only the crops but the people come from other lands. Articles maintained that

1. Nigerians use African artifacts to smuggle heroin into the United States. Most of the heroin sold in Washington, D.C., comes from Nigeria.

2. Jamaicans from Miami and New York go to Washington, where they can control the large open-air drug market.

3. Cars with suburban tags stop in a Washington neighborhood to make buys. This drug traffic incenses the proud, longtime residents there.[37]

Horror stories play a leading role in conventional lore about drugs, but we do not expect newspapers to print them, because so often they are apocryphal. The *Washington Post*, however, wrote about a woman who, after smoking PCP, stabbed a man several times with a butcher knife. Police summoned to her apartment found her standing naked at the window, holding a book in one hand and the knife in the other. Chanting incoherently about Satan, she emerged from the apartment, then stabbed herself in the eye, chest, and abdomen.[38]

These stories would not please liberals or labeling theorists, for they depict users, buyers, and sellers as dangerous, destructive. Reporters may dabble in drugs themselves, but they do not dare write articles on how controlled substances expand their horizons. Instead, pressure is put on them to develop drug horror stories. When Janet Cooke got into trouble and lost the Pulitzer Prize, the moral drawn was that journalists are unreliable. A more appropriate conclusion would have been that reporters are under the gun to discover more and more horrendous examples of the spread of hard drugs (she said she found a child hooked on heroin).

CONCLUSION

What does it mean to say that the media lean to the left on social problems and deviant behavior, and how should such a proposition be tested? One possible approach would be to rely on interviews or questionnaires of reporters, editors, and editorial writers, as Lichter, Rothman, and Lichter did, but this assumes that reporters' personal opinions automatically translate into articles with the same opinions. It may be that reporters keep their opinions out of the news, because of the desire to appear objective or because of pressure on them from editors and publishers not to show their liberal colors in print. Thus, the place to start is with media content rather than reporters.

The most defensible strategy is to turn to sociological theories of social problems and deviant behavior and find which ones lean leftward. Labeling theory clearly fits the description, for it takes the deviant's point of view, criticizes social control officials, and claims that laws are enacted by people in power and enforced against those out of power. According to Howard Becker, who adopts the unconventional sentimentality of labeling theory, the underdogs are always right and the authorities always wrong.[39]

Newspapers could romanticize deviants this way, but they rarely do. The reasons they rarely do are several: (1) reporters usually rely on authorities such as the police for their information on deviance and the people engaged in it; (2) newspaper readers generally believe in conventional morality, which makes them wary of accounts that ignore morality and romanticize deviance; (3) reporters rarely spend enough time with deviants to obtain their side of the picture; and (4) even if reporters were privy to this viewpoint, editors would be reluctant to print it.

The radical view of deviance lies further to the left, and in some ways carries on the tradition of Karl Marx. Newspapers in America are not very likely to adopt explicitly Marxian views of deviance and class struggle. For one thing, reader backlash would be immediate and fierce. To be sure, newspapers nowadays do offer occasional statements to the effect that racism, sexism, and poverty are undesirable and ought to be reduced or eliminated if possible. But these expressions are usually timid and vague.

NOTES

1. Richard Nixon, *Six Crises* (Garden City, NY: Doubleday, 1962), p. 70.
2. Joseph Spear, *Presidents and the Press* (Cambridge: MIT Press, 1984), pp. 54–56.
3. David Halberstam, *The Powers That Be* (New York: Dell, 1979), p. 484.
4. Roger Morris, *Richard Milhous Nixon* (New York: Henry Holt, 1990), pp. 328, 333.
5. Ibid., p. 606.
6. William Safire, *Before the Fall* (Garden City, NY: Doubleday, 1975), p. 308.
7. Edith Efron, *The News Twisters* (Los Angeles: Nash, 1971).
8. Reed Irvine, *Media Mischief and Misdeeds* (Chicago: Regnery Gateway, 1984).
9. Kevin Phillips, *Mediacracy* (Garden City, NY: Doubleday, 1975).
10. Robert Lichter, Stanley Rothman, and Linda Lichter, *The Media Elite* (Bethesda, MD: Adler and Adler, 1986), pp. 22–23.
11. William Safire, *Before the Fall*, p. 360.
12. Russell Baker, *So This Is Depravity* (New York: Washington Square Press, 1980), p. 104.
13. Howard Becker, *The Outsiders* (New York: Free Press, 1963).
14. Edwin Schur, *Radical Nonintervention* (Englewood Cliffs, NJ: Prentice-Hall, 1973), p. 154.
15. Marjorie Williams, "Deaver and the Washington Seduction," *Washington Post*, July 24, 1987, p. D2.
16. Ibid.
17. "Slumlord Serving Time Amid Vermin, Filth," *Philadelphia Inquirer*, July 14, 1987, p. 5-A; Paula Span, "The Public Fall of Bess Myerson," *Washington Post*, July 23, 1987, pp. C1, C8; Vincent Schodolski, "Mexico Community Wants Police to Go," *Chicago Tribune*, July 7, 1987, p. 12; Christopher Hepp, "Officer Accused of Beating Asian," *Philadelphia Inquirer*, July 21, 1987, pp. 1A, 4A.

18. Ron Grossman, "Breaking a Naval Blockade," *Chicago Tribune*, July 8, 1987, p. 2; Sam Smith, "For Doby, the Baseball Scars Are Deep," *Washington Post*, July 7, 1987, p. C4.

19. R. H. Melton, "Scandal Drains Portsmouth of Optimism," *Washington Post*, July 16, 1987, pp. C1, C8.

20. Linnet Myers, "Doctor Gets 10 Years in Sexual Assault Case," *Chicago Tribune*, July 9, 1987, sec, 2, p. 2.

21. Sharon Walsh, "Discrimination Case Against SEC Finishes," *Washington Post*, July 3, 1987, pp. G1, G2.

22. Amy Rosenberg, "Detective Sees Special Rules—and Sexual Bias," *Philadelphia Inquirer*, July 28, 1987, pp. 1B, 2B.

23. David Riesman, *The Lonely Crowd* (New Haven, CT: Yale University Press, 1961); William H. Whyte, *The Organization Man* (New York: Simon and Schuster, 1956); Daniel Bell, *The End of Ideology* (New York: Free Press, 1962).

24. Bonita Brodt, "Victim or Aggressor?" *Chicago Tribune*, July 21, 1987, Tempo sec., pp. 1, 2.

25. Cynthia Gorney, "Cash 'n' Chaos: The Collins Divorce," *Washington Post*, July 24, 1987, p. B2.

26. Len Cooper, "For Crying Out Loud," *Washington Post*, July 9, 1987, p. C5.

27. Rudolph Unger, "Parents Charge Suitor Left Bride at Doorstep," *Chicago Tribune*, July 8, 1987, sec. 2, p. 3.

28. Henry Goldman, "Mother Gets Jail Term in Baby's Death," *Philadelphia Inquirer*, July 10, 1987, p. 9B; Henry Goldman, Robert Terry, and Thomas Gibbons, Jr., "Mother Charged in Death," *Philadelphia Inquirer*, July 29, 1987, pp. 1B, 2B.

29. Linnet Myers, "Raped Girl in Coma; 3 Men Held," *Chicago Tribune*, July 28, 1987, sec. 2, p. 3.

30. Linnet Myers, "Man Gets 60 Years For Attack," *Chicago Tribune*, July 23, 1987, sec. 2, p. 4.

31. Bonita Brodt, " 'I Think of How Much They Cried,' " *Chicago Tribune*, July 23, 1987, Tempo sec., pp. 1, 11.

32. Anne Keegan, "Addicts Worry More About a Fix Than AIDS," *Chicago Tribune*, July 28, 1987, sec. 2, p. 1.

33. Ibid., sec. 2, p. 9.

34. Blaine Harden, "Tribal Customs Worsen Spread of AIDS in Zambia," *Washington Post*, July 3, 1987, p. A29.

35. Richard Powers, "Best of Friends," *Philadelphia Inquirer*, July 1, 1987, pp. 1D, 3D.

36. Cheryl Lavin, "Demystifying the Gay Life," *Chicago Tribune*, July 6, 1987, sec. 2, pp. 1, 2; Lois Romano, "Barney Frank, Out of the Closet," *Washington Post*, July 2, 1987, pp. C1, C10, C11; "Bakker Harassed Male Employees, Former Aide Says," *Washington Post*, August 3, 1987, pp. B1, B6.

37. Nancy Lewis, "3 Sentenced in Nigerian Heroin Connection," *Washington Post*, July 23, 1987, p. B3; Nancy Lewis, "Out-of-Town Drug Dealers Invade Area," *Washington Post*, July 28, 1987, pp. B1, B8.

38. Keith Harrison, "Woman Stabbing Herself Fatally Shot by Police," *Washington Post*, July 16, 1987, p. C3.

39. Howard Becker, quoted by Charles Wright, *Constructions of Deviance in Sociological Theory* (Lanham, MD: University Press of America, 1984), p. 163.

Chapter Six

Columnists on Crime

Before the shots fired at Lexington and Concord were heard around the world, Samuel Adams and several other radical colonial firebrands took pen in hand and composed columns trumpeting sedition. In the same period, Madison, Hamilton, and Jay also turned to column writing. Their eloquent statements would later be collected, and we know them still today as the Federalist Papers. Thus, column writing in the late eighteenth century was nationally prominent and historically significant.

In the nineteenth century, the vitality of newspaper columns eroded, and few columnists from that century are still remembered, aside from Mark Twain and a few of his fellow humorists. In the twentieth century, column writing enjoyed a revival, spurred largely by Walter Lippmann, in some ways a vestigial link to the early columnists. He saw his task not as rehashing or recycling disjointed and perishable bits of news but as offering incisive, trenchant commentary on politics, morality, world affairs, and economics. And this he did for an increasing and appreciative readership.

Lippmann started at the top. Most columnists, on the other hand, began as reporters, which is to say, as news collectors taught to take refuge in minute details and avoid interpretation or critical thinking. Old hands, including editors, warn reporters that descriptive facts are the heart of news, and they discourage those who search for deeper meaning. The transition from reporter to columnist thus calls for abruptly abandoning old habits of fact-centered detachment.

Instead of reporting, columnists get on their high horse and declare war to rouse the apathetic and nonaligned and convert them to their way of thinking. Some can be provocative, as Francis Fukuyama was when he argued that unmistakable changes in communist countries in 1989 signaled an end not only to the cold war but to "history as such: that is, the end point of mankind's ideological evolution and univer- salization of Western liberal democracy as the final form of human government."[1]

While the decline of communism was the top story of 1989, the second major story of the year, according to the *Media Guide*, was crime and drugs in America.

Washington, D.C., was declared our nation's crime capital, but there were few corners of the nation that felt free of the scourge of crack cocaine, the crimes associated with it, and the strains on the social-support and criminal-justice systems. . . . Once reserved for the "Metro" sections or back pages, we found so many regional crimes and drug-related horrors on front pages . . . that we wondered at times if the larger story weren't going unreported, the press scram- bling to cover the battle.[2]

The *Guide* found spot news to be predominant, while serious analysis was comparatively rare.

Columnists are at a disadvantage when dealing with crime, much of which takes place in inner-city slums that they normally avoid. Most of the time, columnists cultivate sources for ideas, and these sources work in the White House or the federal bureaucracy and live in quiet suburbs and commute to work, where patrolling guards offer them protection. The environment of most columnists and their sources thus screens out direct contact with street crime and criminals. In addition, crime and punishment are not the usual metier of a columnist; in most cases it is foreign affairs, domestics politics, or the economy.

Therefore, columnists, when they do write about criminological mat- ters, tend to fall back on personal experience or common stereotypes. When it comes to crime and punishment, personal opinion and unin- formed stereotypes abound; ordinary citizens feel qualified to speak their mind about what criminals are like, what should be done with them, and how well police and judges do their job. This is one of the few subjects where they profess to be experts. (They do not claim such insight into, say, ancient history or nuclear physics.)

This chapter will look at biases in columns dealing with crime. To be sure, all newspaper columns are suffused with values and biases—that is their very nature—for columnists express opinions on turbulent and inflammatory issues to influence readers. It would be a violation of role obligations for a columnist to gingerly sidestep controversy or scrupu- lously present both sides of an issue. The question is not whether col- umnists are biased. It is whether papers are, that is, whether they cling tenaciously to one side, presenting columnists of that persuasion and refusing to print the views of others.

Critics condemn newspapers for their leftist bias. As a test of that argument, this chapter will examine columns on crime and punishment appearing in the 1975 *Birmingham News*, 1977 *Arizona Republic*, 1980 *Seattle Times*, 1983 *Minneapolis Star and Tribune*, 1986 *Providence Journal*, and 1988 *Charlotte Observer*. To measure what ideas are from the left and right sides of the political spectrum, we will turn to Walter Miller's 1973 article on ideology and crime.

His article says the right's crusading issues in the 1970s were that (1) law breakers receive an excessive amount of lenience; (2) their rights and welfare receive careful consideration while those of the victims, police, and ordinary citizens do not; (3) there is too little respect for constituted authority; (4) there is too much permissiveness and relaxation of moral standards; and (5) crime has become far too common and costly. The left largely ignores these issues and crusades instead on the following ones: (1) too many activities have been turned by legislatures into criminal acts; (2) too many people have been tagged as criminal or delinquent by the system; (3) too many have been locked up; (4) criminal justice agencies are too centralized; and (5) such agencies are too biased against particular groups (based on race, sex, age, and income).[3]

Each side emphasizes its particular crusading issues, and the other side ignores them. But on some other questions, both sides confront the same question and simply differ in their answers, for example: (1) Who or what is responsible for crime? (2) How should offenders be dealt with? (3) How should the criminal justice system operate? Unlike the crusading issues, Miller makes fine distinctions regarding these issues, identifying five positions on the right and five on the left, from center to extremes. For example, on question 1, Miller says the extreme left believes that real crime is what those who profit from a brutal capitalist system engage in, while people conventionally termed "criminals" are actually heroic rebels who are defying an immoral social order. The extreme right counters by saying that crime is part of a radical conspiracy to overthrow society.

Columns in the papers from Birmingham, Seattle, Providence, and so on, rather than cover all aspects of crime and punishment, concentrated on a few topics: scandals involving the FBI, the general issue of crime and lawlessness, the need for punishment, the rights of defendants, the wisdom of capital punishment, corruption in the government, gun control legislation, and the problem of illegal drugs. Columnists so rarely touched on other criminological topics that these will not be cited in this chapter, which will emphasize more typical views and subjects.

CRIME AND LAWLESSNESS

Several columnists mourned what they perceived as the collapse of traditional institutions charged with socializing children. They believed

that the increase in crime was due to "the removal of virtually all re-
straints on personal conduct. The decline in parental authority, the erosion of the influence of the churches, the collapse of school discipline
. . . all encourage anti-social behavior."[4] Columnists (with one exception,
Colman McCarthy) refused to blame crime and lawlessness on society's
failure to provide jobs, adequate housing, health care, or living standards. They heartily rejected the idea that economic conditions produce
violent crime. Instead, they emphasized nonmaterial and cultural factors
as the crucial determinants: beliefs, values, and attitudes. According to
these columnists, those who reject conventional values go on to loot,
shoot, mug, and burgle:

The barbarism that rules vast sections of the city when the lights went out is
proof that the Great Society [failed; no amount of government giveaways] can
compensate for the absence of values the home and church provide—a respect
for the rights of others, a personal conscience, religious convictions. When these
internal checks upon behavior are missing, society's only workable safeguard
is force.[5]

Except for John Roche, none of the columnists mentioned how violent
America was in the past. To be sure, no one expects them to cite precise
statistics on murder or assault, for such data are hard to come by but
President Johnson's commission on violence presented ample qualitative
evidence on violence throughout American history. It can be assumed
that columnists were well aware of these reports, for they were publicized widely at the time. Yet columnists seem to have ignored them and
to have embraced the myth that there was once a golden age when
violence was but a rumor—it would become a reality only during the
1960s. That is the implication below:

[Civil libertarians warn about coercive police, but] for most Americans the loss
of rights and privileges we once took for granted hasn't resulted from an unwarranted assertion of police authority. On the contrary, it has derived from a
breakdown in respect for law and institutions, to the extent that the lawless . . .
act upon impulses which, in another era, might have been restrained.[6]

Some columnists concluded that it would be safer to live in a war zone
than near present-day youthful predators.

The FBI reported last week that crime's stranglehold is stronger than ever. Crime
in America is a greater threat than inflation or recession. Crime so pervades
America that a boy is more likely to die by murder than an American soldier in
World War II was likely to die in combat. . . . [We] cowardly cringe as the children
murder, rape and rob.[7]

These fit the conservative mold, according to Walter Miller, who says that the right's crusading issues include (1) the erosion of discipline and respect for authority, and (2) excessive permissiveness. Trends toward increasing permissiveness and immediate gratification undermine homely virtues, such as responsibility and self-discipline, and make crime and deviance more enticing. Individuals whose consciences are atrophying have neither the strength nor the desire to resist temptations.

According to Miller, partisans on the right insist that we need a moral order based on explicit, religious values accepted throughout the society. These moral rules should guide behavior in such realms as sexuality, patriotism, and hard work. Society cannot acquiesce as countercultures promote alternative values, for this would mean capitulating to rebels whose proclivity is to ignore or overturn the wider culture's laws and morals.

Conservatives take an alarmist stance toward crime, which is to say, they view crime as on the rise, as intolerably high, and as potentially threatening everyone in America. Contrary to sociological theorists such as Durkheim and Erikson, conservatives find in crime no silver linings or latent functions. These sentiments show themselves in some of the quotations cited above. When columnists train their sights on crime and lawlessness, they reveal a streak of unabashed conservatism. Judging by Walter Miller, their positions range from slight to medium conservatism (not the extreme variety, which blames today's rate of crime on a radical conspiracy to overthrow society).

DRUGS AND CORRUPTION

Columnists also wrote often about drugs and corruption, though not in the same column. When they devoted columns to the drug issue, they did not dwell on the pushers or the importers but concentrated almost exclusively on the users. Without exception, columnists concluded that illegal drugs harm users directly and the rest of the population indirectly. Despite their consensus on the harmfulness of drugs, they seemed perplexed and ambivalent when forced to consider drug policies (regarding trafficking and usage). William Buckley, for instance, made it clear how infuriating he found the drug problem, then wavered and waffled when he turned to the possible steps to control it.

Coke consumption is up 600 percent in many American cities. In Pakistan, the morning paper advises us, the growth of poppies is up 400 percent over last year. A lot of that stuff is destined for American blood vessels. . . . We are subsidizing a criminal class, overflowing our prisons, . . . and accomplishing nothing. Either bring on the scaffold (which we aren't going to do) or legalize (which we probably aren't going to do).[8]

Buckley's extreme and contradictory solutions remind us of the ancient Roman practices regarding sexual assault. Romans provided two options for the victim of such assault: she could either marry her offender, thus redefining the assault as innocent intimacy, or she could have him executed, in which case the assault was defined as beyond the pale. When the choices differ this drastically, morality deteriorates into something fickle.

While the other columnists who took up the subject of drugs were not as extreme as Buckley, they did betray some ambivalence. One of them (William Safire) conceded that the drug war ought to be fought on all fronts, by which he meant using every means possible from educational programs to baggage-sniffing beagles at major airports. But then he backtracked and changed his message in midcolumn by excoriating congressmen who franticly scramble aboard the drug-abuse bandwagon because drugs are a sexier issue than, say, tax reform, and because this issue will redound to their benefit on election day.

Columns on government corruption were not ambivalent. When corruption reared its head, columnists gave it unstinting criticism, though liberal commentators aimed their thrusts at offenders in the Reagan administration and conservatives blamed everyone else. Consider first a few comments from the right side of the aisle.

Kohlmeier (1975): The smelly fact is that many bureaucrats are up to their knees, navels, and necks in corruption.

Hempstone (1975): With the scales fallen from our eyes [Nixon] can no longer be perceived as the sole dark angel of American politics. . . . [What he did] was in some respects no more than that done by [Roosevelt, Truman, Eisenhower, Kennedy, and Johnson].

More liberal commentators also got in a few shots, some broader than others. Mair complained about the leaders and institutions being selfish, egotistical, and foolish. Nelson and Fain dwelt on the moral failures of the Reagan appointees.

Nelson (1986): In 14 years the instincts of the panicky bureaucracy have not changed. Reagan's men are trying desperately to . . . stop the investigations, invoke that supreme overriding principle—national security—to prevent the world from discovering the truth about their . . . possible crimes.

Fain (1988): Reagan brought to town the shabbiest crew of aides since the Harding administration. The two closest to him, Meese and Mike Deaver, are textbook examples of ethical illiteracy.[9]

THE FBI UNDER SCRUTINY

Of all the criminological topics, the FBI received the most columns. Several times over the years the bureau came under fire for highly suspect activities, most of them instances of excessive zeal rather than corruption—overperformance, not underperformance. In contrast to the columns on corruption, where no one sprang to its defense, in the columns on FBI mischief, the writers were as apt to condone it as to condemn it.

The FBI is one of many federal agencies snooping around in the interests of national security and crime control. While these agencies investigate aplenty, not all of their expeditions have a compelling justification. Take as an example the harrowing experience of the Scientologists. Over a period of 23 years the federal government has

thrown its whole massive weight into a malicious persecution of this religious sect. . . . Millions upon millions of tax dollars have been wasted. . . .
In 1967, the Labor Department harassed the church by denying work permits to visiting ministers from abroad. The CIA checked in. The Post Office brought up its legions of postal inspectors, sniffing for mail fraud. The FBI kept surveilling away. The Immigration and Naturalization Service joined the fun. So, too, did the Bureau of Narcotics and Dangerous Drugs, the Bureau of Alcohol, Tobacco, and Firearms, and the National Security Agency. . . . Finally, the government, having lost at every turn, threw the Internal Revenue Service into the breach.[10]

Columnists riding to the rescue employed several defenses: (1) victims of the bureau, such as the Weather Underground, deserved whatever they received at the hands of the FBI; (2) activities now labeled unethical were previously tolerated or winked at knowingly; (3) spotlighting the misdeeds of the FBI weakens America's internal security and thereby helps the forces of communism; and (4) the American public regards the FBI as a cherished national symbol and thus would be affronted if this organization were given a public flagellation.

Defenders of the FBI took the offense by pouncing on those who cast aspersions on the bureau. Attacking liberals is not something new. Conservative commentators have been engaged in this a long time. The pugnacious Mr. Buckley raised this to an art form, and others followed, so that by now every liberal writer in America, it seems, has had the stake driven though his or her heart a dozen times. For a hint of what the attack mode is like, consider the following:

Fanning the [anti-FBI] hysteria is a curious melange of civil libertarian zealots and outright revolutionaries. . . . [L]egal attacks by such groups in the name of "civil liberties" cripples law enforcement. . . . [W]e can rely upon the vision of juries, self-restraint of prosecutors and political sense of the voters to check law enforcement operations.[11]

How voters, juries, and prosecutors could restrain the FBI remains unclear, since even presidents shriveled at the prospect of confronting the
redoubtable J. Edgar Hoover.

The column on the Scientologists reflects a leftist position, according
to Walter Miller, for it criticizes the law enforcement agencies for their
tendency to intervene, intimidate, and harass people who have not done
anything illegal and have no resources to protect themselves against
federal tactics, technology, and manpower. Many of the columns, however, found what the FBI did commendable. In these columns, writers
often veered far to the right. This is, they assumed that the mission of
police forces is to protect society's law-abiding citizens by calling on the
most modern surveillance and detection equipment to do battle against
the criminals, radicals, terrorists, and subversives in our midst.

RIGHTS OF DEFENDANTS

Defendants' rights are part of a package intended to protect citizens
from the central government. In some cases, Americans came here because they were intent upon securing these rights. In 1773, the Boston
Tea Party angered George III and Parliament, and the British retaliated
by passing what Americans called the intolerable acts (blocking Boston
Harbor and quartering British soldiers in private American homes,
among other things). Years later, writers of the Bill of Rights remembered
these British attempts to curtail rights, and they drew up a list of pro-
hibitions: no religion was to be established; freedom of speech, press,
assembly, and religion were not to be infringed upon; government was
not to interfere with life, liberty, or property.

Fear of the central government trampling citizen rights animated these
writers. It did not occur to them that trampling might result from local
government, but that is what often happened in the nineteenth century,
as local majorities ran roughshod over criminals, blacks, Indians,
women, and the poor, who in many parts of the country found themselves effectively removed from political decision making.

Gradually, the due process clause was interpreted to make most pro-
hibitions in the Bill of Rights apply to the state cases too; some of the
most controversial Supreme Court cases involving rights were decided
in Earl Warren's years. The Reagan administration objected vigorously
to these rulings and called for a rollback; quite a few columnists mur-
murred assent, for the proliferation of rights gave them the vapors,
especially ones granted to the "wrong" people.

Rights multiply like rabbits. Human rights, civil rights, gay rights. . . . Many of
the alleged rights rest on sleight. Take gay rights. Don't homosexuals have
rights? Of course they do. If follows, then, that one has a right to commit

homosexual acts, no? No. Thieves have rights, but it doesn't follow that they have a right to steal. . . . [12]

Tensions between local customs and abstract rights used to be resolved in favor of customs, particular in the old South. Powerful factions used laws to keep others in line. In the modern South the tensions are not always handled in the same way. Take for example the Joan Little case.

It has everything: black vs. white, female vs. male, prisoner vs. jailor. . . . Civil rights groups, women's libbers . . . the Black Panthers and anybody else dissatisfied with his lot [fell] all over each other to contribute money and assistance. . . .
When she was but an unknown burglar, Little had experienced difficulty in retaining counsel. No more: When the time came for trial, she was represented by no fewer than seven attorneys. . . . At a cost of more than $50,000, the defense's 28-member team . . . probed the attitudes of potential jurors [and got a jury ideally suited for its purposes]. Result: After only 78 minutes of deliberation, the jury found Joan Little not guilty.[13]

Several columns revered nineteenth-century thinking, which valued local mores and viewed abstract rights suspiciously. The columnist above said that Joan Little should have been tried in the rural county where the incident took place and not moved to modern Raleigh, where the sanctity of local custom has eroded.

Many columnists wanted to reverse the flow set in motion by the Warren Court, which had established abstract rights benefitting criminal defendants and minority citizens. Traditionalists perceived these rights as a threat to the folkways and prejudices built up by accretion over centuries. According to Walter Miller, this position places its supporters on the right, and not the moderate right but toward the far end of the spectrum.[14]

NEED FOR PUNISHMENT

Philosophers divide justifications for punishment into two basic types: retributive and utilitarian. Retributivists say that people should be punished if and only if they are morally guilty of the wrong committed; and the punishment should be proportionate to the moral seriousness of the offense. They say these punishments are just, right, and fitting, that is, good in and of themselves. Retribution, rather than producing some desirable future change in the offender or society, looks backward in time and says the offender should have to pay for the wrong he or she has done (in much the same way a student is to receive the grade that fits his or her performance in class).

Utilitarians, on the other hand, hold that punishment in itself is not a desirable thing to mete out. Instead, it is something inherently evil and thus should only be used if it has some future effect that more than compensates for this. A number of such possible effects have been spelled out over the years, including special deterrence (striking fear in the heart of the offender, so he or she does not commit the offense again); general deterrence (striking fear in the heart of the rest of society, so people never commit the offense in the first place); and incapacitation (which protects the outside society while the offender is locked up).

We might expect some columnists to show compassion, to discount *all* justifications for punishment and say that prisons are too harsh and dehumanizing to foster any positive changes in inmates. These columnists would go on to say that prisoners in America are locked up far too long and sometimes for behaviors that American legislators should never have criminalized in the first place, because the crimes are essentially victimless. They might further argue that jails and prisons foster alienation and arouse hostility among inmates, making them a greater threat to society once they are let out than they were before going in.

But these positions did not appear in the hundreds of columns I ran across. Columnists of the Will-Buckley-Kilpatrick stripe did not embrace these views, nor would anyone have expected them to, but neither did columnists at the liberal end of the political spectrum. Those who chose to take up the topic of criminal punishment seemed to agree, whatever their stance on political matters, that punishment is desirable. Therefore, columns offered little variety on this topic. The following excerpt does not seem to be something a politically liberal columnist would write, but it is.

Move over, Noah Webster, the recent Claudine Longet trial has just given a new depth and dimension to the word "justice." Miss Longet killed her lover, the world-famous skier Spider Sabich, with a pistol in the Aspen, Colo., home they had shared for two years. A jury found her guilty of negligent homicide. . . .

She was given 30 days in the county jail, which she may serve at her convenience between now and September. Given . . . the fact that a life was taken at her hands, the sentence borders on the ridiculous. . . . Miss Longet begged the judge not to sentence her to any jail time on the grounds that her children thought her innocent and her sojourn in jail would turn them against the system. What a fascinating . . . line of thought!

What about the millions of American children who see that the penalty for negligently killing a human being is 30 days in the bastille?[15]

Now consider what a conservative columnist would say about the need for punishment. Here, I am going to depart from the pattern I have been following, which is to present excerpts from typical or "representative" columns. The passage below is a more intemperate or excessive example from Pat Buchanan, whose fulminations in print go a step beyond the statements of other conservatives.

The objective of the criminal justice system should not be a perfect trial where defense and prosecution are fairly and evenly matched. It should be to establish the truth. . . . And if our present adversary system . . . , hedged about . . . with Warren Court legalisms, is not performing that task, it should be radically reformed or abolished. Even vigilante justice is preferable to no justice at all. . . .

Whether or not the "Son of Sam" took his orders from the neighborhood dog is no more relevant . . . than the fact that Charles Manson thought his orders to start a race war came from a Beatles record. The question of Berkowitz' . . . legal and moral culpability, and the character of his punishment if convicted, should be . . . turned over to the people [of New York].

If Berkowitz, nuts or not, is convicted of murdering those women in cold blood, he ought simply to be given a 50-yard running start—which is more than he gave his victims.[16]

Buchanan comes down in favor of an inquisitorial system, vigilantism, and lynching. He not only holds punishment up as a desirable goal but would sacrifice the rule of law to attain it. This is not the pardonable hyperbole of a person whose words tumbled out before he gave them any real thought. Whether as a columnist or a presidential adviser, he has always tendered this kind of advice.

What matters is not whether columnists tend toward liberalism or conservatism in the generic sense of the terms (experts agree that the columns of today are mostly dominated by conservatives).[17] Instead, the question here is whether they are liberal or conservative in the sense that they say things that fit the criminological models set forth by Walter Miller. Consider position 4 (5 is the extreme) in the models' policies regarding offenders. Number 4 on the left says the criminal justice process is such a brutalizing experience it should be eliminated completely. Number 4 on the right says that dangerous criminals should get the maximum punishment, and it should take place in public, where it might deter any would-be offenders looking on. It seems safe to conclude that columnists who write about punishment have more sympathy with the fourth position on the right than with the corresponding position on the left.

THE DEATH PENALTY

England used to have one of the bloodiest criminal codes in Europe, with 350 offenses punishable by death in the year 1780. Several conditions helped to account for this large number. First of all, property rights at that time were deemed sacred, and merchants then held power in the national parliament. Second, no police departments had been established yet, so political authorities had to rely on the terror of the gibbet to maintain order. In the United States, legislatures never made so many offenses into capital crimes, but many executions were carried out, more than 3,700 during the decades from 1930 to 1960.

Columns devoted exclusively to the question of capital punishment usually opposed the practice (a surprise in view of the overwhelming support columnists showed for punishment in general). Since most Americans approve of capital punishment (at least in the abstract), columnists favoring it did not make a strenuous attempt to convert readers. Instead, they took the wisdom of the death penalty as a given and argued that it should be used more frequently. Thus, Kohlmeier complained that a person has a better chance of being put to death if he drives down a superhighway than if he commits a murder, and van den Haag said that the awful truth of death row is that most inmates die of old age, not electricity.[18]

Proponents saw the electric chair as a tool and therefore something pointless unless put to use. Not a necessary evil. Any qualms they had about the state taking a life they kept well disguised. "[Civil libertarians say] hundreds of people on death row will meet their maker, with resultant suffering and injury to moral decency. It is a threnody we have heard before, grown less persuasive with repeated telling."[19] On the other hand, opponents of the death penalty considered the humanitarian issue paramount, particularly Colman McCarthy, who had this to say about the new, improved methods of slaughter.

Penal officials in New Jersey . . . are deciding that the humane way to execute prisoners is by lethal intravenous injection. By killing them with kindness. New Jersey's executioners reject such harsher . . . methods as electrocution, hanging, shooting and gassing. . . .

In Alabama last April, a malfunctioning electric chair meant that three surges of 1,900 volts of electricity were needed to kill a condemned prisoner. One surge usually does it, but on this occasion . . . a leather strap holding an electrode on the man's left leg burned away. Fourteen minutes of sparks, smoke and flames . . . passed between the first volt and the doctor's pronouncement of death. . . .

New Jersey penologists are seeking to edge away from barbarity. They are really hurtling closer to it. They are not only taking lives but are enshrouding the process in the lie that planned killing can . . . with the proper laying on of trained hands, be humane. . . .[20]

If most columnists oppose capital punishment and invoke humanitarian grounds for doing so, are they then liberal? Miller does not say much about the death penalty, other than that the far right applauds prompt execution of murderers, rapists, armed robbers, and subversives. From this, it is safe to categorize columnists as not belonging to the far right, but that is about all we can say about their "leftness" or "rightness" on this issue.

GUN CONTROL

With about 300 guns for every thousand persons in the country, America, it is apparent, has armed itself to the teeth. The Netherlands, by contrast, has 9 per thousand. American gun control laws are neither very widespread nor very strong. Certainly, they are not very effective in reducing the homicide rate. Maybe they do lower the rate of suicide but with so little research on this question, we cannot say so with any confidence.

In the columns on gun control, opponents of it argued first that it would never work. Then they parted ways and pursued other avenues of thinking: (1) that drugs and Marxism introduced murder into American politics, not hunters or the NRA; (2) that blacks are responsible for the high rate of violence in America; and (3) if guns are placed in the hands of ordinary noncriminals, crime would be deterred.[21] Gun control proponents were no more common than opponents, but their arguments contained greater passion, as in the following excerpt:

More than 20,000 die by pistol fire annually; it is a deadly contagion. In city slums today, homicide . . . is the number one killer of young black men under 24. And . . . 700 policemen have fallen to pistol fire in the last decade.

Are there more shameless triflers with the American public health than the NRA . . . ? No doubt there are lobbyists out there touting relaxed tolerances for rodent dung traces in our cereal. And perhaps some drug company hustler is haunting the corridors of the FDA with the successor to Thalidomide. But they lack the bankroll and blue-chip friends of the NRA, and . . . 20,000 of us aren't dying every year of rodent dung traces.[22]

CONCLUSION

This chapter began with Francis Fukuyama's essay on the end of history, maintaining that the Western idea has triumphed, that ideological challenges to the liberal, democratic way of life are now weak and scattered, and that Marxism-Leninism has been completely routed. (He did not proclaim an end of ideology, however, because that term has come to signify that socialism and capitalism have merged or dissolved. That, he said, has not happened.) Instead, capitalism has continued and thrived while socialism has begun to wither away.

In an odd way the same process seems to be at work in crime columns: the right shows every sign of continuing and prospering while the left has shown more signs of rigor mortis than of vigor. To be on the left criminologically, a writer needs to subscribe to at least one of the following positions:

1. that crime in America is not a serious problem or threat to society
2. that crime control agencies have such arrogance and power that they freely engage in excesses that ordinary citizens find intolerable
3. that ordinary offenders should be granted considerable lenience, and the emphasis in corrections should be on treatment and rehabilitation
4. that long and harsh punishments are immoral and futile.

Columnists tend to view all of these positions with a jaundiced eye. They have no reason to believe that crime in America is uncommon or unserious. What bits of data they receive on the nature of the crime problem may be fragmentary and dubious, but these bits tend to point in the same direction: the crime problem here is serious. Crime control agencies sometimes engage in excesses, but they are not reminiscent of the Star Chamber. There is no Gestapo or KGB-like apparatus skulking about and hounding the typical American. Rehabilitation has its believers (the very term implies its success), but these are more common among the general public than among writers and commentators. In intellectual circles, the rehabilitative ideal has been under fire for more than 20 years. James Q. Wilson has led the assault, claiming that belief in rehabilitation requires us to make heroic and implausible assumptions about our ability to change people's behavior and personality.[23] As for long and harsh punishment, some criminologists may be skeptical about such a policy, but columnists are not criminologists. To most Americans, punishment has intuitive appeal: it seems the natural thing to do. For a serious problem there must be a severe response.

Why don't liberal columnists step forward and disagree with the conservative columnists? On occasion, they do, but there are more conservative columnists in existence, and they are more likely than liberals to take up the topic of crime and punishment. When liberal columnists do write about crime, they do not want to appear romantic or squeamish. Therefore most of them do not betray in print any sympathy for criminals, nor do they suggest that punishment is cruel and immoral. Such sentimentalism is out of fashion and may remain so for the foreseeable future. Softheartedness in matters of criminal punishment now seems to be anything but intellectually respectable. Those who show signs of it are thought innocent, foolish, or brainwashed, as if they had suffered from the Stockholm syndrome.

The overwhelming majority of Americans believe that the crime problem at the moment is extremely serious. In response to grave problems such as this, the tendency of most people is to call for strong, perhaps extreme, solutions. Severe punishment therefore strikes many as perfectly appropriate (whether it actually "works" or not). The call for punishment has been heard; that is one reason why America's jails and prisons bulge to overflowing. What columnists have not mentioned is that this policy has cost a great deal of money without producing a corresponding reduction in the crime rate.[24]

NOTES

1. Francis Fukuyama, "The End of History," *The National Interest* (Summer 1989): 4.

2. Jude Wanniski, *1990 Media Guide* (Morristown, NJ: Polyconomics, 1990), pp. 15–16.

3. Walter Miller, "Ideology and Criminal Justice Policy," in *Aldine Crime and Justice Annual 1973*, ed. Sheldon Messinger et al. (Chicago: Aldine, 1974): 453–473.

4. Smith Hempstone, "Criminality: American as Cherry Pie," *Birmingham News*, April 21, 1975, p. 16.

5. Patrick Buchanan, "Harvest of Permissiveness," *Arizona Republic*, July 20, 1977, p. A–6.

6. Vic Gold, "The Loss of Freedom," *Birmingham News*, January 2, 1975, p. 15.

7. Louis Kohlmeier, "Led by Children of Violence?" *Birmingham News*, April 8, 1975, p. 13.

8. William Buckley, Jr., "Public Hangings for Drug Dealers?" *Providence Journal*, July 17, 1986, p. A–16.

9. Louis Kohlmeier, "Corruption in the Bureaucracy," *Birmingham News*, April 11, 1975, p. 17; Smith Hempstone, "Tracing Roots of Watergate," *Birmingham News*, December 15, 1975, p. 10; George Mair, "American Weathervanes," *Arizona Republic*, July 28, 1977, p. A–7; Lars-Erik Nelson, "Price of a Panicky Bureaucracy," *Providence Journal*, December 24, 1986, p. A–18; Jim Fain, "Meese Should've Never Been Hired," *Charlotte Observer*, April 4, 1988, p. 15A.

10. James Kilpatrick, "Picking on the Scientologists," *Arizona Republic*, August 19, 1977, p. A–6.

11. Eugene Methvin, "Far Left and State Police Bogey," *Birmingham News*, July 11, 1975, p. 13.

12. Joseph Sobran, "Demanding Rights Without Obligations," *Seattle Times*, January 12, 1980, p. 12.

13. Smith Hempstone, "Of Justice and Mockingbirds," *Birmingham News*, October 29, 1975, p. 12.

14. Miller, "Ideology and Criminal Justice Policy," p. 467.

15. George Mair, "Alice-in-Wonderland Justice for Jet Setters," *Arizona Republic*, February 14, 1977, p. A–7.

16. Patrick Buchanan, " 'Son of Sam' Should be Prosecuted," *Arizona Republic*, September 10, 1977, p. A–6.

17. Edwin Diamond, "New Wrinkles on the Permanent Press," *Public Opinion* 7 (April 1984): 4; David Broder, *Behind the Front Page* (New York: Simon and

Schuster, 1987), p. 329; Robert Entman, *Democracy Without Citizens* (New York: Oxford University Press, 1989), p. 31.

18. Louis Kohlmeier, "Supreme Court Will Probably Restore Death Penalty, But It Will Be a Hoax," *Birmingham News*, April 24, 1975, p. 11; Ernest van den Haag, "Protecting the Killers Instead of the Victims," *Minneapolis Star and Tribune*, October 25, 1983, p. 15A.

19. Stanton Evans, "Homicides Doubled in Years of No Executions," *Arizona Republic*, January 26, 1977, p. A–6.

20. Colman McCarthy, "Toward a More Civilized Barbarism," *Minneapolis Star and Tribune*, June 8, 1983, p. 14A.

21. Patrick Buchanan, "Of Guns and Assassins," *Birmingham News*, October 1, 1975, p. 15; Kevin Phillips, "Will Gun Controls work in U.S.?" *Arizona Republic*, March 5, 1977, p. A–6; Kevin Phillips, "Gun Controls Aren't the Answer," *Arizona Republic*, June 13, 1977, p. A–6.

22. Edwin Yoder, "NRA: Taking Aim at Handgun Controls," *Providence Journal*, April 15, 1986, p. A–13.

23. James Q. Wilson, *Thinking About Crime* (New York: Vintage, 1977), p. 190.

24. Michael Gottfredson and Travis Hirschi, "Why We're Losing the War on Crime," *Washington Post*, September 10, 1989, p. C3.

Chapter Seven

Crimes and Criminals

The first three chapters tested a widespread belief that the media wield a great influence over us. Succeeding chapters took issue with the claim that news about crime and deviance slants to the left. While they fastened onto these two issues grimly, critics also entertained several additional beliefs, for example, that crime news is excessive, sensational, and overstated and that coverage of the system (particularly the courts and corrections) has been neglected. It is these additional criticisms that Chapters 7 through 9 will examine.

If newspapers are sensational and given to overstatement in their crime coverage, it is possible that this has some unwanted effects on readers. Conceivably, readers who have to wade through a newspaper saturated with murder and mugging stories each morning after breakfast might become belligerent and mean spirited. On the other hand, they might become resigned and apathetic. This could affect how they react to crime in their own neighborhood.

PUBLIC PARTICIPATION

How people think about crime may be a springboard to action. First consider the Japanese. Early in life they learn what a debt they owe parents and other authorities. This encourages them to obey and cooperate with the police. In addition, in 1963, Japanese citizens formed a network for the purpose of preventing crime. There are more than 400,000 liaison units in it, carrying on preventive actions and reporting crimes to the police as soon as they learn about them.[1]

In the United States we do not have such extensive citizen cooperation with police or a network of units devoted to preventing crime, although in earlier times in America there were a few scattered efforts somewhat comparable to these. When Puritans dominated small settlements in early Massachusetts, they believed that God would punish the entire community for the sins of any individual, so they did not hesitate to barge in on those neighbors they suspected of engaging in questionable activities behind closed doors.

Similarly, farther west, in the mid–1700s and later, vigilantes actively pursued criminals (and sometimes people who were disliked for other reasons). Pioneers took this active role because the formally designated legal officials, usually sheriffs, often proved ineffective in maintaining order in frontier towns. Many vigilante associations drew upon the middle and upper classes for their membership, because businessmen felt they had the most to lose if the town was threatened by an outbreak of crime and deviance.[2]

Today, vigilantes and Puritans no longer occupy center stage in the capture of criminals or the detection of deviants. Nevertheless, American citizens have not completely abandoned their role in the criminal justice system. Police of today are more numerous, and better trained, organized, and equipped than in previous eras, but still they cannot ordinarily apprehend many offenders by themselves—they need the help of citizens if they are going to catch people who break the laws. According to Albert Reiss's observational research of police in the high-crime areas of Boston, Chicago, and Washington in the late 1960s, 87 percent of police mobilizations are citizen initiated, not initiated by the police themselves.[3] Citizens see a crime, call the precinct or 911, act as witnesses once the police arrive in their squad car, and serve as complainants. Later on, if the case goes to court, they may again act as witnesses and testify for the defense or, more likely, the prosecution. Others serve on juries.

With all this citizen participation (and there is far more that I have not cited),[4] we might well argue that the public constitutes an important part of the criminal justice system. And how the public performs its part may reflect its attitudes, opinions, and understandings of the system and the criminals with whom it deals. In turn, these may be influenced by how well the topics are covered by the news media. Therefore, Chapters 7, 8, and 9 will concentrate on the question of how well newspapers cover crime and criminals, courts and corrections.

SENSATIONALISM

Critics commonly complain that crime news is excessive and sensational. Testing such a proposition requires determining first what sensationalism means. While people use the term often, they rarely supply a definition. Hurling this accusation dismissively at papers shows disapproval, but that is about all it shows; it tells nothing about the paper's actual content. For a more serious attempt at definition, we can turn to the *Encyclopedia of American Journalism*, which describes sensationalism as (1) detailed reporting of crime, sex, disaster, and monstrosity stories; and (2) use of emphasis, tone, and language to arouse interest in them.[5] This definition, although seemingly unobjectionable, deserves closer scrutiny.

One way to examine it is by means of examples taken from the *New York Post* of the Rupert Murdoch era, when the *Post* was repeatedly cited as the clearest example of sensationalism in the American daily press. In those years more than a few stories did indeed contain details about sex or crime or both; some of these details may have elicited more than the usual interest from the *Post*'s readers. I will cite a few from minor stories that caught my eye. The first story dwelt on a lawmaker from Sioux City, Iowa, who was charged with indecent exposure following reports of nude dancing at a bachelor party in the Back Forty Lounge in Mingo, Iowa. Another told of a man executed for killing a woman he met at a beach. He removed a thorn from her foot, then took her into the woods, raped and choked her, dragged her back to the beach, where he held her under water, stabbed her, and left her corpse in the river. Finally, an article mentioned a professor at Manhattan's Baruch College who, upon entering a 7–Eleven store in New Jersey, suddenly became incoherent, stripped naked, and poured ice cream and coffee grounds over himself.

What makes these news items engaging is their detail. The location gives the first story its special flavor: the tiny hamlet of Mingo, Iowa, is about the last place we would expect to find a sex scandal. The second story may be gruesome, but the man gallantly removing the thorn from the woman's foot inevitably brings to mind Aesop's fable about the wolf and the ass. We can well imagine the scene in the third story where the professor stands in the middle of the store as ice cream melts amidst the coffee grounds and the mixture runs down his unclad body (Baruch is a well-known business college, and business-school professors do not normally make such spectacles of themselves). In these stories, the *Post* uses evocative details to arouse interest and make the scene come alive. Most books on the art of writing say that this is what writers should do; they would probably praise the *Post* for its colorful details, not condemn it.

Does the *Post* go overboard on crime and engage in sensationalism? To begin, we can compare the *Post* with another paper, in this case, *New York Newsday*. *Adweek* ranks *Newsday* among the top ten papers in the country, which puts it at the opposite end of the spectrum from the *Post*. To see if the obvious is indeed correct (the *Post* carries more crime news than *Newsday*), I counted crime words in each for five weeks in July and August of 1986. The partial results appear below:

New York Post		New York Newsday	
1. Drug	172	1. Shooting	180
2. Shooting	120	2. Drug	166
3. Crack	99	3. Crack	128
4. Died	87	4. Cocaine	99
5. Cocaine	86	5. Murder	90
6. Killing	81	6. Died	85
7. Murder	75	7. Killing	85
8. Robbery	45	8. Robbery	62
9. Beaten	36	9. Wounded	45
10. Drug traff	35	10. Attack	40

The two lists differ only negligibly, for each paper uses the same eight crime words most often, not the result expected when one paper stands near the top of the field while the other constitutes an embarrassment. Moreover, *Newsday* contains more frequent use of crime words. This means that either it practices sensationalism or the *Post* does not—or that word counts do not measure sensationalism very well.

The first two hypotheses seem dubious, so let's consider the third one. If true, this implies that we need alternative indicators of sensationalism. One possibility would be style of headlines, on which the papers do differ. The *Post* favors headlines that stir emotions and appeal to the readers' visceral side, for example, BODY PARTS LINK TO SEVERED HEADS GHOUL PROBED or BRAIN-DEAD WOMAN GIVES BIRTH TO MIRACLE DAUGHTER. Most of the headlines in *Newsday* tend toward the sedate and prosaic. The two papers also differ on the size of headlines. Newspapers ordinarily keep the big block letters out of sight unless something momentous explodes such as world war. The *Post*, however, uses them every day of the week.

Pictures are a third element differentiating the two papers. In the *Post*, front-page photos frequently depict men in the drama of violence or women bursting into tears. This type of photojournalism—that focuses on intense feelings—requires stories to combine raw emotion with personal tragedy. In trying to break into the New York City market, *Newsday* might be tempted to offer the same fare, but as a rule it resists the temptation and sticks to conventional, responsible photos.

In addition, *Newsday* covers noncrime news much more extensively than the *Post* does. Struggling to sell advertising space, the *Post* has a small news hole, about half the size of *Newsday*'s, which means that covering much crime leaves the *Post* with little room for other news. (In that remaining space, the *Post* has been known to gravitate toward the exotic; thus, we might encounter such items as hospital oddities, exorcisms, and crashes.)

These results imply that a new definition of sensationalism should be considered. If, however, the world of journalism wishes to hold on to the old definition, then it may turn out that sensationalism is being unfairly disparaged. A study of Houston news concluded that "the simple fact is that much of value does appear in sensational news coverage," and for some people it is more informative than nonsensational news.[6] This may come as a great surprise but probably it should not, for if sensationalism entails more details, then the natural consequence is more complete coverage.

CRIME WAVES

Sensationalism is routinely disparaged for providing too much detail. Crime waves are also faulted for providing too much information about crime in a short period of time. Some crime waves are not real but the creation of newspaper editors. Lincoln Steffens (who was once a reporter assigned to the police beat in New York) has told of how around the turn of the century a crime wave was created in the newsroom. In the police headquarters, police, reporters, and inmates swapped stories and played cards in the basement. These stories of various escapades, it was understood, reporters were supposed to keep under their hats, not spread around and certainly not put in the papers.

Steffens knew the ground rules, but one day he heard a story he considered too important to keep under wraps, so he shared it with the rest of the city. Afterwards, Jacob Riis, a reporter for a competing paper, was upbraided by his editor for not writing about the incident Steffens had reported. This annoyed Riis, who that afternoon earned a measure of revenge by writing a story based on material stolen from a pigeonhole where reports of major thefts were stored. Then it was Steffens's turn to get chewed out by his editor. When other papers entered the competition by reprinting these articles and adding new ones of their own, the surge in crime news led people to believe that the city was faced with a horde of burglars. Naturally, this came to the attention of police commissioner Teddy Roosevelt, who, being new to his job, feared that perhaps his administration was being overwhelmed by the city's criminal minds. Upon consulting the crime files, though, his assistant discovered that there was no rise in offenses, that the crime wave was just a figment of the newspapers.[7]

In more recent times, sociologist Mark Fishman found that for a while New York media emphasized brutal crimes against the elderly. After a thorough investigation, he concluded:

1. Crime waves include heavy coverage of events that journalists deem part of a theme (such as crimes against the elderly). While most themes are short-lived, a few last longer and constitute crime waves.

2. Journalists learn about crimes by monitoring the police wire, on which police cite crimes they think will interest reporters, such as crime by young punks, crime among strangers, and crime in the street.

3. The media observe each other, and judgments often fan out rapidly from one medium to another.

4. Crime waves build momentum. Reporters who know the crime in question is not actually rising cannot say so publicly, for they are under pressure to ride the wave and cite only evidence that confirms its existence.

5. When the wave catches on, reporters move to the next stage, in which politicians and other well-known figures propose solutions.[8]

In the years since Fishman expressed these thoughts, New York has experienced additional crime waves. The *Daily News* conducted a crime fighters campaign in 1982 to get rid of the city's many rapists, muggers, and pushers.[9] In 1986, newspapers spread the alarm about a crack epidemic and quoted the police commissioner as saying the drug had brought about the loss of an entire generation. By 1990, even the *New York Times* was conceding that the crime problem had gotten out of hand. "By virtually any measure, New York City is [in] a perpetual crime wave, and violence in the city is at an all-time high."[10]

Critics of such reporting say that newspapers have been making strident, irresponsible claims about the extent of crime throughout history (and criminologists tend to agree with this assessment). But before lashing out at papers for overreporting crime, consider this: each year 30 percent of urban households are touched by crime, and only a tiny fraction of these incidents make the news. In view of this, it may be that reporting is more accurate in the midst of crime waves than in ostensibly calmer times (when the lack of crime news implies that crime is practically dying out).

STEREOTYPES

Hardly anyone doubts that people of different religions, nationalities, languages, and races are stereotyped. What may be less well known is that cities, too, find themselves subject to such labeling. New York City, for instance, has long been associated with murders, muggings, and other violence. In the 1750s, observers considered it the most degenerate city in America, and in the 1840s, residents controlled certain neighborhoods with brickbats and cobblestones. There are New Yorkers today who cannot imagine taking the subway train without their stomachs tightening and palms perspiring.

Miami, too, is rumored to have more than its fair share of crime. In 1980 it had the highest murder rate of any city in the world. Drug dealers from competing factions might pull up to a stoplight, notice each other, and pull out their machine guns. It is a city saturated in cocaine and the money used to purchase cocaine: "However you make your money, you know at least some of it has to be drug money . . . . It's on the table when you settle up your bridge scores; it's in the collection plate when you go to church."[11] This has not gone unnoticed; the television series *Miami Vice* broadcast the city's underside to the rest of the country.

Finally, consider the city of Philadelphia, long thought to be suffering from an inferiority complex caused by comparing itself with New York and Washington. Comics picked on it for its stodginess, blue laws, and lack of entertainment. One publication called it a bathroom stop for kids whose parents were driving from New York to Washington. Have the mass media promoted and reinforced these images of New York, Miami, and Philadelphia? One way to find out is by examining the papers in these cities and counting the number of crime words they print.

We have already seen that the *New York Post* and *New York Newsday* use essentially the same crime words with about the same relative frequency. Now consider the *Amsterdam News*, another New York paper, but this one a thin weekly paper written by, for, and about blacks. Given its constituency, the *Amsterdam News* might be expected to delve into different issues than the *Post* and *Newsday* and to include different crime words. The data below show whether this expectation stands up.

New York Post		Amsterdam News		New York Newsday	
1. Drug	172	1. Drug	72	1. Shooting	180
2. Shooting	120	2. Crack	46	2. Drug	166
3. Crack	99	3. Died	31	3. Crack	128
4. Died	87	4. Attack	15	4. Cocaine	99
5. Cocaine	86	5. Drug use	13	5. Murder	90
6. Killing	81	6. Cocaine	11	6. Died	85
7. Murder	75	7. Drug traf	10	7. Killing	85
8. Robbery	45	8. Discrimin	10	8. Robbery	62
9. Beaten	36	9. Shooting	10	9. Wounded	45
10. Drug traf	35	10. Violence	8	10. Attack	40

The *Amsterdam News* shares six of its top ten crime words with both the *Post* and *Newsday*. When the entire word lists are taken into account (instead of merely the top ten), there is a very strong correlation between the *Amsterdam News* and the *Post* (.80) and one nearly as strong between the *Amsterdam News* and *Newsday* (.66). Politically, these papers are miles apart, but in their coverage of crime incidents, they tend to use the same wording and cover the same topics: died, shooting, murder, attack, and killing. These words appear to reinforce the image of New York as a violent place to live in or visit.

But the proposition that newspapers create and support stereotypical images and impressions of their city cannot be tested adequately if the sample is limited to a single city. To get a rough idea of what kind of correspondence exists between the popular image of a city and the nature and extent of crime news in its paper, we should consult three cities at least. Therefore, the data that follow compare New York, Miami, and Philadelphia papers to see if crime words in these dailies reflect the hometown stereotype. That is, do the New York papers offer much more news about violence than the other city papers? Does the Miami paper dwell on drug offenses in greater detail than the other papers? Does the Philadelphia paper offer relatively little crime news as befits a city more stodgy and forlorn than the other two? (Perhaps so, for, according to one criminologist, Philadelphia recently had the second lowest crime rate of any standard metropolitan area in the United States.[12])

Miami Herald		Phil Inquirer		New York Post		New York Newsday	
1. Drug	217	Died	227	Drug	172	Shooting	180
2. Cocaine	159	Killing	173	Shooting	120	Drug	166
3. Killing	127	Shooting	133	Crack	99	Crack	128
4. Died	118	Murder	123	Died	87	Cocaine	99
5. Murder	118	Drug	122	Cocaine	86	Murder	90
6. Shooting	91	Cocaine	90	Killing	81	Died	85
7. Bombing	80	Bombing	65	Murder	75	Killing	85
8. Robbery	65	Violence	65	Robbery	45	Robbery	62
9. Stolen	53	Robbery	62	Beaten	36	Wounded	45
10. Marijuana	51	Injured	60	Drug traf	35	Attack	40

New York is supposed to be a city beset with mindless violence, according to the reigning stereotype. But the *Post* and *Newsday* do not live up to this image of their city, for they do not have more words of violence than the Philadelphia and Miami papers have. Take, for example, the terms killing, shooting, and murder. When we average the *Post* and

Newsday figures, they used the terms 315 times during the period surveyed. The *Miami Herald* used them 336 times, and the *Philadelphia Inquirer* 429 times. If we were to include the term bombing, the New York papers would lag even further behind.

Miami is supposed to dominate the drug traffic in the United States, but this is not the picture presented by the word lists above. Indeed, the terms crack and drug trafficking do not appear in the *Miami Herald*'s top ten crime words, but crack is number 3 on both the *Post* and *Newsday* lists. To be sure, drug words do appear frequently in the *Herald*; they do not appear much more often than in the New York papers, though, so Miami cannot be said to dominate news about drug crime.

Finally, consider the *Philadelphia Inquirer*. There is no crime stereotype associated with the city, so drug crime, violent crime, and crime in general might be expected to have a modest presence in this newspaper. That is far from true, however, for the paper fairly drips with crime, especially violence. Take the terms died, killing, murder, violence, and injured. The *Inquirer* is first among all four papers in the number of times it used these words. This must give pause to those who accuse newspapers of fostering criminal stereotypes for various cities. As far as we can tell, the newspapers are not responsible for New York's violent image, Miami's drug image, or Philadelphia's image as bland and boring.

OFFENDERS

These results do not mean that newspapers do not stereotype *offenders*. It is quite possible that cities are not stereotyped by newspapers but that individuals and groups are. And indeed there are many commentators who say this happens as a rule of thumb in crime news. The media could give excessive attention to the misdeeds of whites or blacks, of the upper class or the lower class, of the young or the old. People from all social categories commit crimes, and some get arrested. According to a leading authority, most crime stories identify offenders as young, male, nonwhite, and under- or unemployed, because police enforce the law more stringently in low-income areas of the city. And news reports reflect this.

The demographic character of the group subject to frequent arrest is a matter of enforcement activities and the concentration of under- and unemployed young males in urban centers such as New York City. If police patrol low-income areas and inner-city commercial districts, the official knowledge produced will register the "fact" that criminals are typically young, male and nonwhite. Crime-beat reporters, relying on police measures and reports, necessarily reproduce these arrest patterns . . . in the reporting of crime news.[13]

Thus, departments assign officers to low-income areas, where they use their discretion to arrest blacks at a much higher rate than whites. Among some academics, this view has become part of the official, or politically correct, ideology in the past 20 years.

Whether it is empirically correct, however, is another matter. The argument could be tested using arrest data on blacks and whites; the FBI supplies figures on this for 29 offenses, the most serious of which are murder, rape, and robbery. Usually police arrest people suspected of these crimes, while for less serious matters (driving under the influence, running away, curfew and loitering, drunkenness) police use their discretion and often let the suspects go free.

If police discriminate by arresting too many blacks, this should reveal itself most in offenses where police have the most discretion, but blacks account for only about 10 percent of the arrests for driving under the influence, 15 percent of those for running away, 16 percent of curfew and loitering arrests, and 17 percent of the arrests for drunkenness. These percentages are not outrageously high, given that blacks make up about 12 percent of the population (and a higher percent of the high-arrest ages, adolescence and young adulthood).

For serious crimes, where police have minimal discretion, blacks have higher arrest rates: 47 percent of forcible rape arrestees are black, 54 percent of murder arrestees, and 63 percent of those arrested for robbery. Thus blacks are most overrepresented in arrests for crimes where police have little leeway: arrest is very likely if a suspect has been caught and probable cause exists. This suggests that police may discriminate less than alleged.

Police can be removed from the measurement process by asking people what crimes, if any, they have committed (self-report studies). These studies have some merits but are usually flawed by including mostly minor offenses and measuring prevalence (percent who have committed the offense at all) instead of incidence (how many times they have committed it). Elliott and Ageton, however, have overcome these flaws, and they have found that for serious offenses (which they call predatory crimes against persons and property), black adolescents admit committing twice as many as white youths admit to.[14]

This leaves victimization data, which, like self-report data, bypass the police altogether. Most victim surveys concentrate on the victims and the offenses they have experienced rather than the offender, which is understandable—since there are many crimes where the victim never learns anything about the offender. Murder and burglary are two examples that spring to mind. But victim surveys concerning crimes such as rape, robbery, aggravated assault, simple assault, and personal larceny do allow the offender's sex, age, and race to be included. John Laub has written an article based on such data in a national survey and

Table 5
Estimated Rates of Rape, Robbery, Aggravated Assault, Simple Assault, and Personal Larceny

	Age		
	12 to 17	18 to 20	21 plus
White Males	7,900	16,000	4,000
Black Males	38,000	74,200	17,700
White Females	2,000	1,200	300
Black Females	6,900	4,500	1,400

has estimated the rates of offending per 100,000 in several age/sex/race categories (see Table 5).[15]

For these five crimes at least, it would appear that black males commit crimes at a higher rate than white males. The difference between the two races is not as pronounced among women, but it is still about three to one. This is another bit of evidence that seems to suggest that the racial difference in arrests may be not merely a reflection of police bias.

In claiming that police discriminate whenever they arrest relatively large numbers of people who are black, young, male, and under- or unemployed, critics imply that police decisions to make an arrest are entirely their own or that these results are due to police deployment of troops (more in minority areas). When police overpatrol low-income neighborhoods, they will inevitably observe more crime and make more arrests there. But, as noted earlier, Albert Reiss and his associates found that citizens initiate most police mobilizations and, as witnesses or complainants, they tell police what to do with the suspect. Moreover, police usually go along with their wishes, a finding that also hints that differences in arrest rates for various groups may not be entirely due to police discrimination.

If there is a strong relationship between race and engaging in predatory crimes, why? Frankly, criminologists do not know, though they occasionally offer speculative hypotheses. One is that blacks have less to lose if they are caught and sent to prison.

Doing time was not a troubling event in this world, or even terribly newsworthy. A brother would disappear from the street, and people would say, "Aw, the ole boy's in jail," as matter-of-factly as if were away visiting a maiden aunt. . . . Doing time didn't scare him; the joint was like the projects, except they feed you free.[16]

Needless to say, this overstates the case considerably, and does not describe the great majority of black Americans.

Finally, do reporters faithfully reproduce police arrest patterns when reporting crime news? There are several reasons for doubting it. First of all, not all arrests can be written up in the newspaper, for space limitations prohibit it. New York City has 2,000 murders and many more rapes a year, but few of them make the news. Second, those that do make it often involve someone of wealth, power, prestige or fame. For the have-nots of society, being a victim rarely brings such media attention. For the poor and minority, crime is a daily presence largely overlooked by the press.

A 29-year-old woman goes to the top of a 21-story building to watch a sunrise. There, two armed men rape her and force her to jump from the roof. She grabs a television cable that miraculously breaks her fall. She holds on, naked and screaming, until residents of the building save her life. The story makes the inside pages of New York's newspapers. Life in the city goes on.

Weeks later, a 28-year-old woman goes out for an evening jog. She is beaten, gang-raped and left for dead. She clings for life until help arrives but lapses into a coma and hovers dangerously near death. Every new development in the case is faithfully chronicled and official New York is mobilized in outrage. . . .

Why does one story so fascinate the news media and the public while the other quickly vanishes? . . .

One woman is from Harlem, the other from the Upper East Side. Those facts alone influence how they will be covered.[17]

Doris Graber has examined some of these issues in her study of crime in the Chicago newspapers. She counted the number of offenders whose race was mentioned in the papers to see if crime articles greatly overrepresented blacks. In 1980 Chicago was 40-percent black, a percentage below Washington, Atlanta, and Detroit but higher than most other cities. Therefore since blacks accounted for 55 percent of the murder arrests in cities across America in 1980, the figure should have been higher than that for Chicago. But it was not higher in Chicago newspapers. Graber found that blacks made up only about one-eighth of the racially identified offenders. Was this a sampling fluke? Apparently not, for in New York, Miami, and Philadelphia papers, I found that in those instances where the race of the suspected offender could be determined (either from the words or the pictures), whites outnumbered blacks by the same ratio as Graber found in Chicago newspapers, that is, seven to one.

As for youths, many commentators (including James Q. Wilson) have pointed to them as the main perpetrators especially of violent crimes. Some have said that they are the primary persons identified by newspapers as offenders. Again Graber's Chicago data deal with this question. She divided offenders mentioned in the papers into three age groups, the young (under 25), the middle (25 to 35) and the older (over 35). She did not find that the young outnumbered the other two groups when offenders and their ages were given in the crime articles. In fact, the group mentioned most often was the older one. The young did not even come in second place, for they had fewer mentions than the middle group. I studied this issue using the New York, Miami, and Philadelphia papers, grouping offenders' ages by decades. In doing so, I found few of them to be in their twenties. In fact, there were more offenders in their forties—and in their fifties!

In real life a great many offenders are under- or unemployed, but is this true of offenders whose job status is mentioned in the newspapers? Not according to Graber's findings in Chicago. She found that the *Tribune* gave the following occupational designations to offenders:[18]

Bureaucrat, professional, or business manager	62%
Skilled or unskilled labor	15%
Unemployed	11%
Student	8%

New York, Miami, and Philadelphia papers did not contain such precise designations as bureaucrat and professional, so I relied on somewhat cruder classifications: (1) middle or upper class, (2) lower class, and (3) unemployed. Using this method, I found that 80 percent of the suspects and defendants whose wealth or occupation was mentioned fell in the high-status category and 18 percent in the low-status category. Only two percent were identified as unemployed. Hence, these data provide even stronger refutation of the argument that crime articles dwell on unemployed offenders. My conclusion is that most newspapers do not assign too much coverage to crime by the male, young, black, and under- or unemployed portion of the population. It could be argued that, except for males, these offenders are actually underrepresented.

CAUSAL THEORY

If readers are to be well informed about crime and criminals, if they are to learn enough to make sound decisions when asked to vote for different crime policies, they need help from the news media. They need some insight into the causes of crime. They will not likely receive help from television, so newspapers must come to their assistance. Do they? Not according to Graber. She says that few crime stories are analytical or evaluative. Few delve into the thicket of causation. Instead, readers must supply their own interpretation. In general, papers ignore the causes of crime; when they do not ignore them, they tend to go astray (citing mental illness or simple greed). This failure is not inevitable, though. As an example of what can be done, consider this piece:

Many Indians assign economic causes to bride-burning and blame difficult times for its apparent increase. In a nation of 755 million people, there are only 24 million wage-paying jobs, and the number of unemployed people in the cities and with education is growing. A government clerk earns about $950 a year. An income of $2,000 puts a family firmly in the middle class.

And meanwhile, the government's new economic program has made available consumer items that were unimaginable a few years ago—kitchen gadgets, tape decks, sporty cars. In that climate . . . "dowry is the shortest cut to acquisition"— and two dowries a seldom-prosecuted path to even more. But others say the deeper cause is a culture that offers women few options outside marriage and little comfort within it. Indian marriages are still arranged and brides still live with their in-laws. . . .

"You don't expect love," . . . and indeed the ties between mothers and sons are traditionally much stronger than between husbands and wives in India. In a match founded on a financial arrangement . . . a young bride has "neither love nor family bonds" for protection.

But neither does she have many options if a marriage turns brutal. Few women can support themselves; only one in four can even read. And Indian families are reluctant to take back their married daughters. "They have paid a dowry; they feel they have done enough". . . .

India's legal system seems only a faint deterrent to bride-burning. New Delhi police have brought murder charges in 143 burnings in the past 2 1/2 years, but in only 16 cases have there been any convictions.[19]

This *Wall Street Journal* article focuses on a type of crime instead of an isolated incident, thus allowing the reporter to seek expert opinion (not that of the patrolman on the scene) and to explore wider issues such as India's economy and culture. After reading the article, it is hard to imagine any analysis of bride burning that would omit such cultural issues as how marriage and family relations there are conducted and organized. The causes uncovered may seem disparate, but they all have in common the fact that they isolate brides and make them vulnerable to more powerful men. The article gives no simple answers such as greed and insanity. It goes much deeper. If other papers covered crime as well as the *Wall Street Journal* in this instance, the improvement would be dramatic.

CONCLUSION

Earlier studies of crime in the news often compared the *New York Times* with the *Daily News* and assumed that all other papers in America resembled either of these models, either eminently respectable broadsheets that shunned street crime or low, cheap tabloids that emphasized mob hits and dismemberments. The problem with such an assumption is that the *New York Times* is unique and scarcely resembles other papers. Unlike the *Times*, most broadsheets cover crime extensively, even more than the tabloids (because of the larger news hole).

Tabloids such as the *Daily News* are routinely accused of appealing to prurient interest by printing sensationalism, a term sometimes defined as detailed news about crime that excites reader interest by coverage that is too vivid or thorough. Critics, gravid with taste and concern, apparently would prefer crime to be written of in pro forma manner, like obituaries (which in a sense some crime stories are). A closer look would reveal that crime news these days does not delve into the grossly offensive such as cannibalism, disembowelments, and the like. And most stories are devoid of color and stylistic embellishment; instead they usually follow the dry formulas taught in journalism schools.

Critics denounce crime waves, too, again because they represent a perceived excess of crime news. In this case it is not too much detail in one story but too many stories—with which newspapers imply or state overtly that crime is rising rapidly and getting out of hand. Critics object to this kind of journalism because it is often misleading, for usually the crime rate has not experienced a radical burst at all but has remained the same.

Such criticism may be apt in many cases, but there is another side worth mentioning. Newspapers cover only a small fraction of actual crimes. Furthermore, American crime is pervasive. New York City, for instance, now has about 2,000 murders a year, and it is not even close to being the city with the highest rate. Crime waves are said to give the impression that we live in a dangerous and crime-ridden society. That impression is hard to quibble with. Indeed, it is practically indisputable.

Critics also fault crime coverage for stereotyping cities. Thus, stories of crime in New York, it is argued, portray that city as caught in a spiral of senseless violence, while news stories about Miami suggest that its fame rests on its status as a haven for drug dealers. Philadelphia, on the other hand, has been stereotyped as a stodgy outpost where nothing very exciting happens. Although newspapers and other media are charged with spreading these stereotypes, the data do not back up the accusation, for the *Philadelphia Inquirer* prints the most crime and violence news, while the New York papers provide the least.

Finally, complaints surround the coverage of suspects and defendants.

Criminologists, at least some of them, say that police arrest the poor and minorities discriminatorily and newspaper reporters follow the police lead and write an inordinate number of crime articles about such persons. In fact, editors practice triage. They must screen the many crimes and casualties of crime, because resources are limited (such as space), and only a few of them make the news. In the sorting, crimes at a fancy address are most likely to make it, not some rapist who attacks women in the slums.

When critics' laments about sensationalism, crime waves, stereotypes, and the like are converted into measurable concepts and testable hypotheses, what seemed so obvious and incontrovertible turns out to be less so. The news about crime does not fit these categories or obey these propositions as neatly as heretofore imagined. Thus, the standard criticisms of crime coverage have a way of greatly exceeding the empirical evidence or even ignoring it.

NOTES

1. William Clifford, *Crime Control in Japan* (Lexington, MA: Lexington Books, 1976).

2. Samuel Walker, *Popular Justice* (New York: Oxford University Press, 1980).

3. Albert Reiss, Jr., *The Police and the Public* (New Haven, CT: Yale University Press, 1971).

4. Roy Lotz, Eric Poole, and Robert Regoli, *Juvenile Delinquency and Juvenile Justice* (New York: Random House, 1985).

5. Donald Paneth, "Sensationalism," *Encyclopedia of American Journalism* (New York: Facts on File, 1983), p. 451.

6. Richard Hofstetter and David Dozier, "Useful News, Sensational News," *Journalism Quarterly* 63 (Winter 1986): 853.

7. Lincoln Steffens, *The Autobiography of Lincoln Steffens* (New York: Harcourt, Brace and World, 1931).

8. Mark Fishman, *Manufacturing the News* (Austin: University of Texas Press, 1980); Mark Fishman, "Crime Waves as Ideology," *Social Problems* 25 (June 1978): 531–543.

9. Steven Gorelick, " 'Join Our War': The Construction of Ideology in a Newspaper," *Crime and Delinquency* 35 (July 1989): 421–436.

10. Todd Purdum, "The Perpetual Crime Wave Crests and a City Shudders," *New York Times*, August 1, 1990, sec. B, p. 1.

11. T. D. Allman, *Miami: City of the Future* (New York: Atlantic Monthly Press, 1987), p. 65.

12. Georgette Bennett, *Crimewarps* (Garden City, NY: Doubleday, 1987), p. 77.

13. Drew Humphries, "Serious Crime, News Coverage, and Ideology," *Crime and Delinquency* 27 (April 1981): 198.

14. Delbert Elliott and Suzanne Ageton, "Reconciling Race and Sex Differences in Self-Reported and Official Estimates of Delinquency," *American Sociological Review* 45 (February 1980): 95–110.

15. John Laub, "Data for Positive Criminology," in *Positive Criminology*, ed., Michael Gottfredson and Travis Hirschi (Newbury Park, CA: Sage, 1987), p. 67.

16. "Brothers," *Newsweek* (March 23, 1987): 73.

17. Ellis Close, "Rape in the News: Mainly About Whites," *New York Times*, May 7, 1989, p. E27.

18. Doris Graber, *Crime News and the Public* (New York: Praeger, 1980), p. 57.

19. June Kronholz, "Lingering Cruelty," *Wall Street Journal*, August 21, 1986, pp. 1, 16.

Chapter Eight

Reporting on the Courts

Press coverage of the courts has been decried for years, as scholars and members of the bench and bar bemoan reporters' ignorance of the law and emphasis on trivia and personalities. No one states this more bluntly than Lyle Denniston: "As the legal profession sees the press, it is often a journal of superficial impression and petty horrors, addicted to imprecision and to exaggeration, gullible and yet inattentive, careless to the point of irresponsibility."[1]

It might seem that courts would be full of promise as a source of news. In fact, they tend to be disappointing much of the time, in part because they do not seek publicity. Rarely do judges or lawyers grab reporters in the hall and try to impose their views upon them. Professional norms discourage this kind of assertiveness. And courts have not established press offices for disseminating information to reporters. In this hesitancy to use the media, courts clearly do not follow the pattern set by the other two branches of government.

Another obstacle to court reporting is complexity; a trial certainly is not as simple as, say, a fire or an accident. Court cases go through a series of stages, and they hinge on questionable facts and esoteric legal issues; it is always disputable whether there is proof enough to satisfy a judge or jury. In some instances, the testimony in court bogs down in technical disputes among expert witnesses, and none of this translates easily into plain English for the ordinary reader.

Translating legalese into something readable can be particularly difficult when the court reporter does not understand the crucial legal points on which a case may hinge. Many reporters assigned to the courts are neophytes with little experience in any kind of news coverage and

none at all in court coverage. Most court reporters are not legal specialists; few have gone to law school. Even those with such legal training
have much to learn, because law schools do not prepare students for
the criminal courts and their informal behind-the-scenes maneuvers.

Covering the courts does not mean simply sitting inside a courtroom
all day, taking notes furiously and giving a full account of the testimony
in the next day's edition. That model prevailed in the nineteenth century
but has disappeared in the late twentieth. Today a reporter may have
to cover 15 or 20 courts instead of one, and only three or four hours to
spend on them during the day. The other time will be logged on the
computer, typing up notes and fashioning them into a printable article
or two. This means that reporters spend their early hours scurrying from
one office to another, conversing with clerks and conferring with police,
lawyers, and occasionally judges in search of leads, pointers, quotes,
and interpretations about what is important, what has happened, and
what could happen next.

Therefore court reporters normally set foot inside an actual courtroom
only rarely and even then perhaps for just a minute or two. No one
these days takes court testimony verbatim like a legal stenographer. This
may seem extraordinary, like a sports reporter who never goes to the
ball park to watch a game, but the nature of the beat seems to require
this.

Critics of court reporting say the faults begin with reporting that is
shallow and superficial, incomplete and misleading, because the journalist has a feeble understanding of the court. Second, the amount of
reporting given to the courts is so small; days may go by without any
news of what is happening in the courts, and then only a paragraph or
two. Third, critics decry the emphasis on spectacular, heinous crimes
that reporters dramatize shamelessly to build interest and circulation.
This threatens the right of the accused to a fair trial, as in the following
two cases.

DEHUMANIZING

When police found ransom money on Bruno Hauptmann in 1934 and
arrested him for murdering and kidnapping the Lindbergh baby, the
press seized on this and would not be appeased until Hauptmann was
convicted and executed, a series of events that it helped bring about. In
those days, most cities had several competing newspapers, and reporters
felt intense pressure to develop fresh leads. They routinely resorted to
breaking and entering, planting evidence, photographing it, stealing
pictures, and so on. Reporters and editors found these to be amusing
adventures; it was the first thing rookies learned.

Tom Cassidy, allowed into Hauptmann's apartment, thought it would be a lark to plant some incriminating evidence, so he opened one of the closet doors and wrote in pencil the telephone number and address of the man who had offered to serve as intermediary between the Lindberghs and the kidnapper (whose identity was unknown). On the door jamb, he wrote "$500" and "1928" and the serial numbers of two dollar bills. Then he smudged the numbers as if someone had tried to wipe them off. Cassidy was not alone in trying to make Hauptmann hang. Hearst's *New York Journal* circulated reams of fiction: that maps in Hauptmann's apartment included roads near Lindbergh's secluded home, that the chisel on Lindbergh's lawn was one missing from Hauptmann's set, that Hauptmann's shoe matched a print found below the kidnapped baby's window, and on and on.

The trial drew a throng of reporters and commentators, including Alexander Woollcott, Damon Runyan, Dorothy Kilgallen, Heywood Broun, and Walter Winchell. Succumbing to the hysteria, they rained abuse on the defendant, saying that on the stand he seemed

completely devoid of human characteristics, his face blotched, his mouth sagged, his eyes avoid all the other eyes that stared at him. He made senseless denials. He laughed pointlessly. I found myself thinking that the creature must be insane, and then I began wondering if this too were not a carefully calculated pose, if, when a point came when there was no answer . . . Hauptmann would not leap and scream, and rave, posing as an out and out madman.[2]

Hearst hired and paid the defense lawyer, just to get a pipeline of information. The lawyer never doubted Hauptmann's guilt, barely talked to him, and defended him incompetently (having general paresis rendered the lawyer virtually senile).

With the trial little more than a formality, its conclusion was never in doubt. Alexander Woollcott said that the only people who had not formed an opinion had to be congenital idiots or Tibetan Lamas. Nevertheless, one after another on the panel of potential jurors claimed to have no fixed opinion on the case. Although sequestered, jurors were quartered in the same hotel as many of the commentators, who during breakfast each day referred to Hauptmann as "the Nazi monster" and "the baby killer." Soon afterwards he was convicted and quickly put to death.

THE SNOWBALL EFFECT

Thirty years later, Marilyn Sheppard was murdered in her sleep in Bay Village, a distant suburb of Cleveland. Dr. Sam Sheppard, her husband, said he got up from the couch where he was napping and checked on her because he heard a noise. When he looked in, he was beaten around the neck by an unidentified man. Officials never pursued leads on other suspects, so Sam Sheppard was the only one under consideration, and evidence against him was negligble, insufficient to justify arrest.

Louis Seltzer, editor of the *Cleveland Press*, stepped in when the Sheppard case seemed on the verge of fizzling out. Seltzer knew how to wield power; several mayors and governors owed their positions to his influence on Ohio's voters. He did not hesitate to throw his weight around, usually to great effect. He faulted police for not capturing the murderer and attacked them with pointed front-page editorials, all of which demanded that Bay Village officials go after Sam Sheppard. Eventually, officials did as they were told, and public opinion was galvanized. The editorials Seltzer used to goad police into action included this one.

Maybe somebody in this town can remember a parallel for it. The Press can't. And not even the oldest police veteran can, either. . . .

From the morning of July 4, when he reported his wife's killing, to the moment, 26 days later, Sam Sheppard has not set foot in a police station. He has been surrounded by an iron curtain that makes Malenkov's Russian concealment amateurish.

His family, his Bay Village friends—which includes its officials—his lawyers, his hospital staff, have combined to make law enforcement in this county look silly. . . .

Gentlemen of Bay Village, Cuyahoga County, and Cleveland, charged jointly with law enforcement—

THIS IS MURDER. THIS IS NO PARLOR GAME. THIS IS NO TIME TO PERMIT ANYBODY—NO MATTER WHO HE IS—TO OUTWIT, STALL, OR IMPROVISE DEVICES TO KEEP AWAY FROM THE POLICE OR FROM THE QUESTIONING ANYBODY IN HIS RIGHT MIND KNOWS A MURDER SUSPECT SHOULD BE SUBJECT TO—AT A POLICE STATION.

The officials throw up their hands in horror at the thought of bringing Sam Sheppard to a police station for grilling. . . .

A murder has been committed, you know who the chief suspect is. You have the obligation to question him . . . from beginning to end, and not at his hospital, not at his home. . . . [3]

During the drawing of names of potential jurors (veniremen), reporters stood by, and, unaccountably, officials released the names, which papers printed. Readers then deluged the panel members with unsolicited opinions. Forty times during the trial, newspapers included pictures of the individual jurors, meaning the community would long remember them if they rendered an unpopular verdict.

While the *Cleveland Press* led the assault on Sheppard, papers as far away as Los Angeles made the case their top story. During the trial, reporters made themselves conspicuous, 20 of them sitting at a table inside the bar where they were not more than three feet from the jury.

Entering and existing the court at will, they sowed confusion and disrupted testimony. They made such a ruckus and leaned over to eavesdrop so often that Sheppard and his attorney could not confer.

If members of the jury held strong opinions from the outset, so did the judge. According to an interview that Dorothy Kilgallen revealed years afterward, the judge had believed that Sheppard was "guilty as hell." Spurning judicial principles, he gave interviews about the case on the courthouse steps. (He was up for reelection). To no one's surprise, the jury declared Sheppard guilty, and the judge gave him the maximum—life in prison. A decade later the case wound its way to the Supreme Court, which ruled that the trial had been flagrantly unfair. In a retrial, the prosecution's case collapsed, freeing Sheppard (but by that time he had deteriorated physically and mentally, and he died a few years later).

FAIR TRIAL AND FREE PRESS

Had a handful of people read one article and formed a half-hearted opinion of guilt, that could easily have been overcome by trial testimony. But in these two cases many newspapers printed many biased articles, spread many false accusations, offered many blatant headlines and retouched photos. Publicity reached avalanche proportions; no one could have halted it if he or she had had the inclination. Defenders of the media say that such indiscretions are few, and even these few instances of irresponsible journalism have no effect on the outcome. In fact, however, jurors are swayed. Benno Schmidt says that publicity sometimes saturates a community "with a preconception of the defendant's guilt, and inflames passions for vengeance to such an extent that the capacity for discriminating, individualized justice may be overwhelmed."[4]

The American Bar Association points to six kinds of publicity that harm defendants. Newspapers have been urged not to put these bits of information in their write-ups. Just how cooperative they have been can be determined from a 1979 study of 29 papers. The findings below show what percent of the papers violate the rule in question.[5]

RULE	PERCENT
Reference to test results (fingerprint, polygraph)	2
Admissions, confessions by the accused	12
Prior criminal charges or convictions	13
Statements about witness testimony or credibility	24
Opinions about evidence, chance it will appear in trial	25
Opinions about accused's character, guilt or innocence	35

Over two-thirds of the articles break one of the rules, suggesting that as a continuing policy papers routinely undermine defendant rights.

Does this have any effect on juror decisions? To see, Padawer-Singer and Barton took jurors from regular jury pools, gave them an audiotape of a real case to listen to in a real courtroom, then sent them to a jury room for deliberation. Eighty percent of those exposed to prejudicial clippings beforehand voted to convict. People not exposed were evenly split among guilty and not guilty votes. In another version, using voir dire, the differences were even greater. Research has shown that the more people know about a case, the more prone they are to vote guilty. Those who read local newspapers know the most about cases.[6]

COURT NEWS

If indeed most Americans depend on the press for information about how the criminal courts operate, then we might ask about the kind of court coverage the press provides. Does it allow the person who reads the daily paper's court news religiously to acquire much insight into the nature of the system? Critics, particularly lawyers and judges, seem to think not, accusing the press of imprecision, superficiality, and exaggeration, of ignoring wider issues while focusing narrowly on individual cases.

So say some critics. Testing their hypotheses requires determining what the wider issues of criminal courts are. A number of possibilities might be suggested. The following list strikes me as as good as any:

1. Traditionally, judges have wielded immense power in the court. Though most of them are prosecution-minded, the public has perceived them as lenient and liberal. Legislators, aware of the public clamor, have sought to curb some of the judges' power by limiting their discretion in sentencing. Legislatures have passed laws aimed at reducing both lenience and disparity.

2. Indeterminate sentencing had once been the norm. It allowed judges considerable leeway; they could impose short sentences or long ones, whichever they saw fit in a particular case. And parole boards, if they deemed the inmate to have reformed, could set him or her free long before the sentence had been completed. This formed a key element of the rehabilitation philosophy.

3. Courts in large cities experience excessive congestion. High crime rates (especially violent crimes), personnel shortages, and excessive numbers of continuances lead to overburdened staffs, rapid personnel turnover, and burnout. And a huge backlog of cases. Some go to trial years after the original incident.

4. Courts act as funnels, which is to say, the number of cases at intake dwarfs the number of persons who get sent to prison at the end of the process. About 10 percent receive that disposition. Somewhat more go to jail. Many

more receive probation. Most have their cases dropped or dismissed without a trial or a guilty plea.

5. Most people accused of a serious crime elect to plead guilty instead of going to trial. For this cooperation they normally receive a favor in return, either a reduction in the charges or a reduced sentence. By choosing not to go to trial, the defendant saves the court enormous amounts of time and money.

6. This is not to say that trials are insignificant. America is the only country that has a large number of jury trials. And whether it is a jury trial or a bench trial, it will be watched closely by prosecutors and defense attorneys. They take into account the verdicts and sentences of other cases when deciding what they should do in their present case: whether to plea bargain and what kind of bargain to strike.

7. Public defenders handle the majority of cases—not private defense attorneys—because most defendants are indigent (in large cities, indigent minorities). Courts are constitutionally obligated to provide a legal defense. Public defenders receive for their perhaps heroic efforts modest pay and appreciation. Neither the public nor their clients like them much. The latter view them as far less competent than private attorneys (an accusation that research into the matter disputes). Hostility from one's clients fuels the burnout rate among PDs.

8. Like judges, prosecutors exercise great power. They decide which cases to discard and which to pursue. Normally they drop those where evidence is insufficient, where the actual harm caused is relatively minor, or where witnesses prove to be reluctant, uncertain, incredible, or "unfindable." Prosecutors decide which cases to try, which ones to bargain in, and which to drop. They also dominate grand jury decisions and influence bail and sentencing.

9. The most difficult decision facing judges is sentencing. They usually recognize that jailing or imprisoning offenders tends not to have a very salutary effect on them and may lead to irreparable damage. Judges normally rely on the presentence report; drawn up by the probation officer, this documents the present offense, the offender's prior record, and his or her personal and social background and experiences.

10. Criminal courts are essentially powerless to resolve the nation's crime problem. They cannot put every offender behind bars or in a treatment program that works. They cannot undo the problems plaguing most offenders. Where family, school, church, and economy have failed, the court cannot step in and right an individual in a five-minute hearing over legal questions.

How well do the newspaper articles on the courts cover these points? To answer that question, I examined 20 newspapers for the month of November 1989 (excluding Sunday issues): *Albuquerque Journal*, *Arizona Republic*, *Atlanta Constitution*, *Burlington* (Vermont) *Free Press*, *Charleston* (South Carolina) *News and Courier*, *Charlotte Observer*, *Cincinnati Enquirer*, *Daily Oklahoman*, *Deseret* (Salt Lake City) *News*, *Detroit News*, *Fargo* (North

Dakota) *Forum, Great Falls* (Montana) *Tribune, Honolulu Star-Bulletin, Indianapolis Star, Kansas City Times, LA Times, Philadelphia Inquirer, Portland* (Maine) *Press Herald, Rochester Democrat & Chronicle,* and *Washington Post.*

1. *Judges tend to be prosecution-minded, but the public generally views them as lenient and liberal. Poll-reading legislators have reacted to the clamor of constituents by trying to reduce sentence discretion.*

While none of the news articles on the courts said explicitly that judges have awesome power or lean toward the prosecution, they implied it in a number of examples of extremely severe sentences: "The total sentence, imposed by Texas District Judge Gerry Meier, was four consecutive life terms, plus 70 years and a $75,000 fine. 'We do things a little different down here,' Lawrence Mitchell, a Dallas lawyer who is handling Saul's appeal, said Tuesday. 'This is a tough, tough county.' "[7] Actually, harsh sentences are not a monopoly held by judges in this county. Consider this article that concerns a different state: "A judge Wednesday told an admitted rapist, 'I'll do everything I can to keep you off the streets,' then gave him 16 consecutive life terms. . . . [He added], 'You have forfeited your right to ever be a free citizen. . . . [Unfortunately, this crime] doesn't carry the death penalty.' "[8] Why do American judges resort to such harsh penalties when no murder is involved? Why do they side with prosecutors on many issues decided by the court? One reason is that for years the general public thought judges too often relied on technicalities of procedure or tenderhearted compassion to set defendants free. Not wanting to lose office in the next judicial election, after a while many judges began to get tougher on defendants.

Public pressure does not completely account for the way judges handle cases. America has a long history of severe punishments, including the death penalty. Colonial laws, drawing on Biblical sources, prescribed capital punishment for such minor matters as defying one's parents. Legislators nowadays rarely cite Biblical precedent, but they still put faith in stiff penalties. They may assume that the person committing the crime is a hardened, vicious or career criminal instead of an amateur acting on a momentary impulse.

Penalties in the United States are harsher than elsewhere. In Norway, the minimum penalty for rape or for sexual intercourse with a child under age 14 is one year behind bars (no one gets four consecutive life terms as the man in Texas received). In West Germany, robbery nearly always brings less than five years. Very few robbery convictions in the United States produce a sentence this light. Newspapers do not mention how drastically American sentencing patterns differ from those in the rest of the world.

Several attempts have been made to reduce sentencing discretion and disparity. California, in the forefront of innovation, has abolished parole and gives judges three sentencing options for each particular offense.

If the lightest penalty is selected, the judge must spell out the mitigating factors. The aggravating factors must be proved in court if the judge is to assign the heaviest penalty. Not surprisingly, most judges choose the middle course.

Some newspaper articles mentioned mandatory sentences, and one went into detail on sentence disparities, which are one reason why legislatures passed mandatory sentencing laws.

Virginia's circuit judges have voted overwhelmingly to establish statewide sentencing guidelines after a one-year experimental program significantly reduced sharp fluctuations in sentences. . . .

The guidelines grew out of a study [showing that] sentences could be influenced by a defendant's sex, race and socioeconomic status or . . . by which judge happened to be sitting behind the bench.[9]

Thus judges also want uniformity, as this article indicates.

2. *For years judges wielded considerable power, particularly in sentencing. Parole boards also had power; they could release inmates from prison long before their nominal sentence was served. The indeterminate sentence constituted a crucial element in the philosophy of rehabilitation.*

Promoted by Progressives, indeterminate sentencing enjoyed a vogue in America. They considered punishment inherently evil and required that it be administered only if it brought clear benefits, such as rehabilitation. This progressive philosophy of criminal justice focused on the individual, not his or her offense. The person would receive expert treatment: his or her psyche would be probed, the underlying problem diagnosed, and a treatment regimen prescribed. (It is obvious why this has been called the medical model.) When cured, the patient would be released from the program or institution, and it was assumed that he or she would go forth and sin no more.

Progressives viewed rehabilitation as the only justification for punishment and believed that once this goal was reached, the person ought to be freed. Someone familiar with the inmate's progress therefore had to have the power to release him or her. Judges were too far removed from the scene for such a task; parole-board members seemed more appropriate for they at least talk with prisoners periodically.

The rehabilitative ideal held sway for a long time before coming under fire from several quarters. Robert Martinson dealt a major blow to the ideal; he and his colleagues examined studies evaluating individual therapy, group therapy, milieu therapy, education, training, and medical procedures and found that not one of these consistently reduced recidivism. This conclusion alarmed treatment professionals, who launched a counterattack against Martinson. All this ferment and controversy in the field animated criminological discussion for years. News articles in

November 1989 did not refer to it (perhaps they had mentioned it in years past).[10]

3. *Large urban criminal courts find themselves clogged with an excessive number of cases. The staff members are overburdened with work, and many of them elect to quit after a few years on the job rather than continuing to suffer. Cases get delayed time and again by lawyers, resulting in a huge backlog that worries court administrators (who want cases pushed through expeditiously).*

Criminal courts in large cities stagger under increasingly heavy caseloads; this is a predicament that court reporters have shown some interest in, several articles mentioning it in passing, and one pursuing it in detail. The latter was in the *Washington Post*, a paper where we expect problems to be examined in depth. The following is an excerpt:

Prosecutors who try the most serious murder cases in D.C. Superior Court told their boss . . . last month that "critical" shortages of staff and resources leave them "one step ahead of disaster."

The extraordinary meeting was the latest and most acute sign of distress in a criminal justice system that has been strained to the breaking point by the District's raging homicide rate. Similar pleas for help have been raised in recent months by the city's trial and appellate judges, D.C. police and the Public Defender Service. . . .

It is not uncommon for a murder case to take a month in trial and require a prosecutor to develop dozens of witnesses and exhibits. Prosecutors interviewed this week spoke of rape and murder cases being neglected for months, with investigative trails growing cold and witnesses' memories dimming, as the prosecutors scrambled to meet court deadlines in other cases.[11]

There were at least subtle hints of this in other articles, as many reports routinely cited dates, including when the offense occurred. All the articles sampled were written in November 1989, but the offenses typically took place in 1988, one of them as far back as 1985. Thus readers were not informed explicitly of the innumerable delays, clogged calendars, and burgeoning caseloads, but for those who read between the lines to ferret out subtle facts, there were clues. Hence, they might have suspected that backlogs existed and guessed at what problems accompanied such backlogs.

Trained to concentrate on one case at a time, reporters normally say very little about the courthouse regulars or courthouse working group (judge, prosecutor, defense attorney, et al.). They dwell mostly on the offense and the major developments in the case at each stage in the proceedings. Courts can be shadowy institutions, and to understand them better, citizens need to know something about the understandings, routines, and recurring problems that form the backdrop for the court's decision making. Newspaper reporters rarely answer this need with pertinent insights.

4. *Criminal court cases are sifted and funneled: far fewer cases emerge at the end (sentence) than existed at intake. Not many individuals make it all the way from charge to prison. Many more find their way out of the maze at some point, often by dismissal, or if found guilty, by probation instead of a fine or incarceration.*

American courts are extremist: both very lenient and very harsh. They tend to give no punishment worthy of the name or one that is cruel and excessive. The Supreme Court could stop this but has chosen not to, for severity has become an accepted element of the system. In 1980, for instance, in *Rummel v. Estelle*, the Court said that Texas could put an offender away for life if he or she has been convicted of three felonies, which might seem all right in the abstract, but hapless Rummel's misdeeds were not heinous ones: using a credit card fraudulently, passing a forged check, and obtaining money by false pretenses. In all three of these cases, the money involved was a piddling amount.

European courts do not do this. They punish nearly all defendants but not severely. In the United States, half the felony arrestees are diverted or dismissed before there can be a trial or guilty plea. Of those that remain, nearly half will be found guilty, but most of them will receive probation, a punishment found risible by some offenders, for whom it is about as effective as a note sent home to their mother.

News accounts sometimes point out that a case has been dismissed or that a convicted offender has been put on probation instead of sent to jail or prison. They do not say how many cases receive this kind of disposition. Nor do they mention that for every thousand felonies committed in the United States, only six people will be sentenced to prison for more than one year. Reporters do not emphasize either of the criminal justice system's primary qualities: the tendency toward extremes in punishment and the funnel effect. But they do provide a number of examples for the very observant reader to ponder.

5. *Most individual offenders convicted of a felony do not have their case tried before a judge or jury. Instead, a great majority of them plead guilty after bargaining with the prosecutor for some considerations (since by pleading guilty, they are doing the harried prosecutors a favor).*

As noted already, for every hundred felony arrests, only half go very far in the courts. The other half are rejected, diverted, or dismissed by the prosecutor. Nearly all of those that remain in the courts result in guilty verdicts, most of them due to guilty pleas rather than trials. Pleas keep the assembly line running and save money. They outnumber trials ten to one in state and local courts.

Critics denounce plea bargaining. Some (such as Albert Alschuler) say that it forces defendants to give up their basic constitutional rights and protections, including the presumption of innocence. They add that judges and prosecutors have an incentive to accept plea bargains, but it is always possible that at a trial the defendant might be found not guilty. Other critics fault plea bargaining for permitting defendants to plead to charges milder than those of the actual crime. This leads to lesser penalties and suggests that the system has fallen to the level of a Middle Eastern bazaar.

Plea bargaining in big-city courts relieves congestion and saves time and money, of course, but it also serves other purposes. Defense attorneys often lack the resources to pursue a case to trial, so they, too, may seek to bargain. Prosecutors may want a guilty plea because it is a sure thing. Trials are not, for sometimes surprises are sprung that scuttle the prosecutor's case; witnesses may fail to appear or remember, or may change their testimony in midstream. Prosecutors adopt the bird-in-the-hand philosophy: they prefer a conviction with a mild sentence to taking a chance on a more severe penalty at trial but also risking a not-guilty verdict.

Defense attorneys usually have a weak case, because the best defense cases have already been dismissed or rerouted by the prosecutor. The remaining defendants are considered guilty by the courthouse regulars, so the focus normally shifts from the question of guilt to the question of what sentence best fits the defendant. Defense attorneys therefore must work for the lightest sentence they can get. This usually means foregoing a trial, because individuals found guilty at trial may be penalized more severely than if they had gone along with the guilty plea. This is known as the trial penalty.

Court reports in the newspaper do mention plea bargaining in cases. I found well over a dozen stories that used the term "bargain." Several of them said that it was struck because the defendant had agreed to testify in other cases as a witness. In one instance, an article noted that the bargain was completed in the interests of justice and fairness.

On Tuesday a defense lawyer revealed that the sisters have struck a plea bargain. [They] pleaded guilty to involuntary manslaughter and, in exchange, the prosecutor agreed to ask the judge to sentence them to no more than a year in county jail. . . .

[T]he prosecutor said that a stiff punishment is not appropriate in light of the circumstances surrounding Ariza's death. "We're convinced these women did not mean to kill him. But they did a very, very stupid thing, and should have to pay a penalty for it."[12]

6. *Trials may not be especially common but they are important. Prosecutors and defense attorneys observe the verdicts and sentences and use these as a baseline in deciding whether to take their cases to trial and, if not, what to ask for in the bargaining talks with the other side.*

Prosecutors and defense lawyers know, above all, that most cases that go to trial end in guilty verdicts, although the rate varies from crime to crime. James Levine's research on federal juries found that about 80 percent of trials lead to conviction in cases of national defense, selective service, immigration, and food and drug violations. For cases where the offenses involve anti-trust, civil rights, or migratory birds, however, guilty verdicts are less than half that high.[13] State and local court juries tend not to convict when they think the probable sentence too harsh.

Cases go to trial when the bargaining sessions break down, and they do so for a number of reasons. Sometimes the defendant is adamant about being innocent and will not consider pleading guilty, even though it would be in his or her interest to do so, for the evidence against him or her is strong. Other times the prosecutor refuses to offer a modest sentence, so with a severe penalty staring at them anyhow, the defendants take a chance on a trial and hope for an acquittal. In some instances, the prosecutor does not bargain, because the press has made the case a celebrated one, and the public, its interest whetted, insists on a trial to resolve the crime.

Court stories in newspapers do not bring these points to their readers' attention. The fact that trials, though comparatively infrequent, bear heavily on the calculations of prosecutors and defense attorneys gets passed over in news accounts of trials and plea bargains. The fact that some defendants turn down plea bargains out of sheer stubbornness is never noted by the press. This is in keeping with journalistic practice: do not try to explain that which has not happened (in this case, the plea bargain). Just stick to what has happened.

7. *Indigent minorities constitute the defendants in most cases in urban criminal courts. Not able to hire their own, they get assigned public defenders, who receive little remuneration from the government and practically no respect from their clients (who almost reflexively perceive them as uncommitted and incompetent). After a few years on the job, public defenders may succumb to burnout.*

The Gideon and Argersinger cases decided by the U.S. Supreme Court require that attorneys be provided for indigent defendants. Large cities normally comply with these expensive requirements by supplying public defenders (smaller counties tend to rely on assigned counsel). Millions of court cases per year in the United States keep public defenders busy. With up to three-fourths of defendants in large cities indigent, the PDs' caseloads overflow.

Money may be just one of many resources that these defendants lack. Often they are undereducated as well, having gone to inner-city schools and not graduated from high school. Their knowledge typically does not derive from textbooks idealizing the courts as a bulwark of liberty and constitutionalism. Instead, it is likely to be based on casual comments on the street that exude cynicism (according to which, judges and lawyers deserve as much trust as hustlers and junkies).

Nevertheless, indigent defendants still retain an element of unrealistic idealism, for regardless of their guilt, they tend to believe that a truly competent lawyer will be able to win for them a not-guilty verdict in court. They ordinarily regard anything less as a failure on the part of the lawyer—even a guilty plea to a misdemeanor, when the original charge was a felony. Usually the evidence against them is compelling, and therefore they have little likelihood of gaining an acquittal. The cases where the defense has a good chance of winning usually have already been weeded out by prosecutors, who do not want to risk losing at trial.

Public defenders draw cases that are difficult to win and clients that are difficult to like. Sullen, smoldering with resentment, they may not trust or cooperate with their lawyers. Other clients may be willing but unable to cooperate, because they cannot understand simple instructions. Some cling to incredible alibis. Some believe that you get what you pay for (and they pay their public defender nothing).

How effectively do newspapers convey this information? Three stories described homeless or transient suspects, hence presumed indigent. Another detailed the case of a defendant who said that he had no money and needed a large amount to put up an adequate defense. One article quoted a private defense lawyer saying that public defenders are inexperienced and overworked. Finally, a reporter characterized Montana's public defender system as a mess that required a thorough reorganization.

Court stories gave defense attorneys little attention and rarely identified them as public defenders. Perhaps the clients were wealthy and hired private attorneys, or perhaps the lawyers were public defenders and this fact simply went unmentioned in the account. Or both of these may have been at work in the stories.

8. Prosecutors wield great power, deciding which arrests to pursue and which to drop, which cases to bargain in and which to try. They dominate grand juries and influence bail and sentencing decisions.

Although charged with prosecuting all crimes, prosecutors have the option not to do so, and no one is peeking over their shoulders, second guessing their decisions. Relations with all parts of the system, from police to corrections, is one more reason for their widespread influence. Their discretion is immense.

Some prosecutors have a pro-police bias, some do not. Others have a more legalistic bent. When a prosecutor decides not to proceed on a particular case, police may curse and grumble, but there is little they can do about it, for the case cannot be resuscitated. Judges and defense attorneys accept most decisions that prosecutors make—they are not subject to review.

If they crack down on one type of crime and ignore others, prosecutors rarely announce these policies publicly. Historically, police blamed judges but now they see the prosecutor's hand in such decisions and dislike it. Prosecutors also have a jaundiced view of police work, accusing police of making arrests but failing to build a strong legal case. Unwilling to risk losing in court, prosecutors usually dismiss cases where the evidence or witnesses are shaky.

Newspapers give prosecutors considerable attention, often depicting them as bent on extracting the maximum penalty possible. One prosecutor interviewed hoped to win a conviction and obtain a death penalty, while others expressed anger when the verdict was not guilty or the sentence not severe enough. Articles treated prosecution and defense as locked in mortal combat, while they ignored the prosecutor's other responsibilities—for example, trying to move the pile of cases and taking care of business as expeditiously as possible.

9. Judges' most difficult decision comes at the sentencing stage. Most of them now realize that jail and prison time do little good for most inmates and sometimes immeasurable damage. In deciding what sentence to impose, judges often rely on the probation officer's presentence report, which details the crime, prior record, and background of the offender.

Sentencing can be agony. Giving a light sentence means that the offender might soon go out and commit a heinous crime. Giving a more severe sentence might ruin any chance the offender had of rehabilitation. Judges have no ESP, no ability to peer into a defendant's future. Newspapers do not touch on the difficulty of passing sentence or the anxiety that judges feel. Nor do they cover the presentence report and recommendation. Often, the sentence just seems to happen. Passive constructions give the impression that the offender received a sentence, not that the judge actively chose it: "A California woman who was the mastermind of a fraudulent-bond scheme that cost the federal government about $450,000 in Arizona and a host of private companies nearly $1 million, was sentenced Monday to nine years in prison."[14]

10. Criminal courts may be largely powerless to resolve America's crime problem. They cannot put every offender behind bars. Nor can they undo the everyday problems afflicting most offenders. Where family, school, church, and neighborhood have failed for years to exert a beneficial influence over the individual, it is scarcely imaginable that five minutes in front of a harried judge will accomplish more.

The American culture has traditionally taken a can-do, optimistic approach. Presidents such as Roosevelt, Kennedy, Johnson, and Reagan exuded confidence in what America could do. The only requirement was a desire to solve the problem, and Yankee ingenuity would see to it that it got "fixed" (that quintessentially American word). Few writers go against the grain and say that nothing can be done, the problem is insoluble. One of those few in criminal justice is Paul Wice, who wrote:

The criminal courts have always been a dumping ground for society's misfits and losers. People who, because of mental, physical, educational, or socioeconomic deficiencies, cannot succeed in the legitimate world, become the clientele of the criminal courts. . . . The criminal courts have no direct impact upon those societal and psychological forces thought to be responsible for the development of this criminal class.[15]

It should come as no surprise that newspaper articles on the courts do not take such a dim view. Maybe journalists cling to the view that all problems can be solved. Maybe they think the criminal justice system as presently constituted is the best possible solution. Or maybe they do not really give the question a second thought. Instead they leave it up to the commentators and pundits. Whatever the reason, court coverage does not address the most important question of all—does the system work?

WHAT DOES RECEIVE COVERAGE

Newspapers cover these ten points but not well. We thus know what court reports do not do, but what is it that they do do? First of all, they tend to recreate the crime. They may do so at any point in the case, from the arrest to the sentence. Sometimes papers eloquently describe the offense, the scene as it developed, and the actors' reactions. This represents a substantial improvement over what passed for court reporting just a few years ago, which typically involved little more than naming the legal offense. That was not helpful, for many legal terms were arcane. What, for instance, does the ordinary reader know about malfeasance or reckless endangerment?

Court reporting in the daily newspapers tends to cover some kinds of crime heavily and virtually exclude other kinds. Murder stands out as the most prominently featured crime, along with attempted murder. More stories are devoted to it than to any other offense. There are several reasons for this. First of all, most people see it as the most serious crime in existence. Second, murders often lend themselves to storytelling, particularly if the people involved are relatives or have close ties.

Drug offenses constitute a second front in the war on crime, judging by the number of court cases listed in the newspapers. Not all the cases take place in the large cities of the East or West Coasts, where we might expect them to. Some occur in cities and towns where drug dealers would not be expected at all. The following account refers to the heart of Mormon country, where caffeine and nicotine are viewed with suspicion—making cocaine beyond the pale.

America's war on drugs came home to a cocaine kingpin Thursday when U.S. District Judge David Sam sentenced Orestes Luciano Abreu to 33 years in federal prison and fined him $20,000.

In 1988, Abreu, a Miami resident, was arrested in Salt Lake City and a semi-automatic assault rifle and a revolver were seized. . . .

In September, he was stopped at a routine roadblock in Mississippi and arrested with three-quarters of a kilogram of cocaine. He was returned to Salt Lake City for trial and convicted on seven counts: conspiracy, possession of cocaine with intent to distribute it, four gun charges, and escape.[16]

When such a case lands in the courts of Salt Lake City, novelty alone makes it big news.

In addition to court cases involving murder or drugs, newspapers often cover those dealing with sex crimes. These seemed evenly divided between rape cases where the victims are adult women and other sex violations where children are the victims. The nationally famous McMartin preschool case was the best-known instance of the latter; in November 1989 it was winding down after two and a half years in court. In addition, newspapers devoted a number of articles to children as the victims in nonsexual crimes. Some of these were neglect or abuse cases (of a nonsexual kind), such as the following:

Four-year-old Kimberly McZinc starved to death in a mobile home on a dirt road here in the Florida Panhandle. The refrigerator was stocked with food. Four other children in the home were plump and beloved.

Kimberly's mother, a college graduate with a master's degree in public administration, is gripped by twisted fundamentalism.

She believed that her spunky little girl was possessed by demons.

To exorcise the evil, she denied Kimberly food and made the weakened child run "with Jesus."

. . . Nicholson had powers and "talked to God," [Kimberly's mother] said. And Nicholson told her that God said Kimberly was possessed by demonic spirits of disobedience, gluttony, lust and lying. Fasting and punishment were the cures. Nicholson took control of Kimberly's diet and discipline.[17]

Newspapers may have spotted a trend, for court cases involving victimized children are on the rise.

Finally, news accounts cited cases where the purported offender was someone in the criminal justice system or in some position of power or prestige, such as judges, lawyers, police, high government officials (Oliver North, Richard Secord, John Poindexter), bank owners and other financiers, contractors, ministers, and large corporations. Reporters seem to take special delight in pointing out the misbehavior of people in the criminal justice system—once they have been caught.

CONCLUSION

At one time the press gave the courts more extensive coverage than it gave the police, but that is no longer true. Courts are thus not covered as much as they could be; in addition, researchers have not given much attention to how the press covers the courts. The majority of research in this area focuses on the fair trial/free press dispute. In this area, the press deserves the criticism directed at it and more. Newspapers continue to violate American Bar Association guidelines regarding confessions and prior records of defendants. While coverage does not wallow in the excesses of the Walter Winchell era, it still routinely violates the rights of suspects.

Aside from the fair trial/free press debate, do news media cover the courts adequately? Most critics, especially lawyers and judges, complain of omissions, distortions, and misinterpretations. They fault the press for covering the courts on a case-by-case basis, which means overlooking the larger issues of the legal system. To test how valid this proposition is requires determining what the larger issues are—on which there may not be much consensus, for lawyers and criminologists have quite different conceptions of them. Each has his or her own interpretation and his or her own high standards, which newspapers generally fail to meet.

News media stress events of the past 24 hours, while critics want them to adopt a more historical or sociological approach, and to devote attention to the inner workings, informal organization, and back regions of the criminal court instead of merely reciting what decisions were reached in open court. This chapter has shown that newspapers do cover some of the larger issues; they just do not cover them as thoroughly as critics would like.

The failure of court reporting to meet these standards has been defended by Ericson, Baranek, and Chin, who argue that "far from omission, selection and distortion being problems for the news, they are fundamental to the news process of envisioning order and influencing change."[18] This may be letting the press off too easily, by suggesting that it is the very nature of the institution to cover the courts this way. This is probably an overstatement, for not all court coverage contains such flaws (see the *New York Times*) and coverage has changed over the years.

A more apt response to the failure would be to ask whether *any* writing meets the standards set by the critics. Editors do not assign reporters the task of presenting the critical issues confronting criminal courts of today, so reporters fail to provide such a summation. On the other hand, criminologists sometimes do have this mission, and they, too, often fail. That is, when called upon to set forth the main problems or issues besetting the legal system, they do not cover them completely or accurately. Only a handful of books, such as Paul Wice's *Chaos in the Courtroom*, can be said to give a very good exposition of most issues.

Most criticism of court reporting was written some years ago, that is, at a time when such reporting tended to dwell on names of defendants, to imply that defendants were guilty beyond all doubt, and to simply give the legal name for the crime and expect readers to understand what happened. But recently, court reporting has shown considerable improvement, going beyond mere names and legal terms to provide more description of the events and circumstances surrounding them. There is no gainsaying that court news still fails to provide analysis or critical thinking, but it deserves some credit for the small gains it has made.

NOTES

1. Lyle Denniston, *The Reporter and the Law* (New York: Hastings House, 1980), p. 6.

2. Ludovic Kennedy, *The Airman and the Carpenter* (New York: Viking, 1985), p. 204.

3. Louis Seltzer, "Why Isn't Sam Sheppard in Jail?" *Cleveland Press*, July 30, 1954, p. 1.

4. Benno Schmidt, "Nebraska Press Association: An Expansion of Freedom and Contraction of Theory," *Stanford Law Review* 29 (February 1977): 451.

5. James Tankard, Kent Middleton, and Tony Rimmer, "Compliance with American Bar Association Fair Trial-Free Press Guidelines," *Journalism Quarterly* 56 (August 1979): 467.

6. Alice Padawer-Singer and Allen Barton, "The Impact of Pretrial Publicity on Jurors' Verdicts," in *The Jury System in America*, ed. Rita Simon (Beverly Hills, CA: Sage, 1975).

7. Betsy Gerboth, "Saul's Attorney to Appeal Sentence," *Fargo Forum*, November 1, 1989, p. C1.

8. Nolan Clay, "16 Life Terms: Judge Puts Rapist Behind Bars," *Daily Oklahoman*, November 23, 1989, pp. 1, 2.

9. Patricia Davis, "Sentencing Guidelines Endorsed," *Washington Post*, November 19, 1989, p. C1.

10. Robert Martinson, "What Works?—Questions and Answers About Prison Reform," *The Public Interest* 35 (Spring 1974): 22–54.

11. Barton Gellman, "Prosecutors Cry for Help to Share Murder Caseload," *Washington Post*, November 9, 1989, pp. B1, B11.

12. Jerry Hicks, "Plea Bargain Reached in Manslaughter," *Los Angeles Times*, November 1, 1989, p. A22.

13. James Levine, "Using Jury Verdict Forecasts in Criminal Defense Strategy," *Judicature* 66 (May 1973): 448–461.

14. Susan Leonard, "Mastermind Gets Prison, Told to Pay Restitution in Bond-Fraud Scheme," *Arizona Republic*, November 21, 1989, p. B4.

15. Paul Wice, *Chaos in the Courthouse* (New York: Praeger, 1985), pp. 163–164.

16. Joseph Bauman, "Cocaine Kingpin Gets 33 Years in Prison," *Deseret News*, November 17, 1989, p. B1.

17. Celia Dugger, "Mother Starved Girl to Exorcise Demons," *Arizona Republic*, November 8, 1989, p. A1.

18. Richard Ericson, Patricia Baranek, and Janet Chin, *Negotiating Control* (Toronto: University of Toronto Press, 1989), p. 90.

Chapter Nine

Reporting Life behind Bars

While few commentators mention how the media cover prisons, those who do generally agree on two critical points: that the press hardly attends to prison life at all and that what coverage there is usually concerns outbursts such as escapes and riots. After reading these repeated assertions, a person might think that they must be right. I did. But both propositions have been called into question by James Jacobs, whose content analysis of the *New York Times* and *Daily News* of 1976 found that they did not ignore prisons. The *Times* ran nearly 500 articles and the *Daily News* over 360 that year—far more articles on prisons than on most topics.

Perhaps these results were skewed; 1976 might have been an exceptionally newsworthy period in correctional matters. Therefore I consulted the New York Public Library's computer list of newspaper abstracts for the period of January 1989 to August 1990. It showed that the *New York Times* printed 636 articles and editorials in that period that were devoted to prisons. Like Jacobs's research, this indicates that prisons are not ignored by the newspapers.

Jacobs also took up the question of whether prison news articles are dominated by stories about escapes or disturbances. He used a particularly broad definition of disturbance, one that included inmate rape, riot, and similar violence but also such things as illegal contraband, suicide, guard brutality, strikes, slowdowns, and sickouts. Despite the expansive definition, disturbance stories were not the main topic of prison news; they made up only 11 percent of the items. Far more common were media treatments of penal policy and prison conditions (particularly in the *New York Times*) and celebrities (particularly in the

Daily News).[1] When I examined the 1989–1990 prison articles in the *Times*, I found very few of them devoted to rioting or similar inmate outbursts.

Why do prisons receive rather extensive coverage when commentators claim they get little? Richard Ericson and his associates offer the hypothesis that prisons are relatively closed to the media except in communities where prisons are dominant.[2] In Canada, where Ericson lives, prisons may not be very numerous, but in the United States we have prisons in many places, because most prisons hold fewer than 500 inmates and there are more than 750,000 state prison inmates (as of June 30, 1990). This does not count the many jails, federal prisons, camps, halfway houses, and other correctional facilities.

There remains one more criticism: that newspapers tell us little about the nature of life behind bars. It could be argued that papers ought to do so, since citizens spend a large part of their tax money to build new facilities and to maintain those that already exist. Word has it that it would be cheaper to send someone to Harvard than to Sing Sing, which is a sobering thought and a challenge to prisons to do something that justifies such expenditure.

This chapter will begin by setting forth two sociological models of prison society, the importation and deprivation models. It will then question both, because in recent years prison violence has grown apace, making life for some inmates solitary, poor, nasty, brutish, and short. Next, we will examine how thoroughly the news media reflect the new reality of life behind prison bars.

PAINS OF IMPRISONMENT

Donald Clemmer spent several years during the Depression at Menard, a maximum security prison in southern Illinois, after which he wrote a classic sociological treatise on life among prisoners. That was the era of the big house, which is to say, the prison with large cell blocks housing mostly poor whites. It was typically rural, isolated, and inaccessible; mail and visitors were discouraged. The daily routine was rigidly enforced, with much discipline and hardly a gesture at treatment. Above all, custody was the watchword.[3]

Clemmer said that inmates new to prison, upon first entering, found it intimidating. Some of them, stripped of their outside identity, never fully recovered an equilibrium, while others socialized with fellow inmates, learned the informal rules, and joined the inmate culture. He called this taking on of convict norms, values, and beliefs "prisonization." One of the primary norms, which prisoners were instructed in immediately, was to despise and distrust the enemy: prison guards, higher-level administrators, and the parole board.

At that time, 60 years ago, Illinois laws were particularly punitive, leaving inmates at Menard and other prisons throughout the state with long sentences to serve. These prolonged stays inside the walls made it likely that inmates would shed their pre-prison attitudes and values and become readily assimilated into the convict subculture. Furthermore, once they became fully prisonized, Clemmer hypothesized, they would not adapt very well upon being set free. More likely, they would go back to committing crimes and getting in trouble, then return to Menard or some other state facility.

While Clemmer's work covered a wide range of issues, Sykes and Messinger focused more narrowly on the theme of prisonization and inmate culture and sharpened it considerably. They insisted that society not only isolates inmates but rejects and condemns them as dangerous outcasts. While behind bars, prisoners find themselves closely guarded, stripped of all human comforts, and reduced to subsistence level. In addition, the absence of women means no heterosexual contacts are possible. This deprivation causes some men to begin doubting their own masculinity.

Sykes and Messinger said that prisons take away individual autonomy; they regulate the daily existence of prisoners by insisting on a multitude of rules covering sleeping, eating, working, talking, and going to and fro. These impose a new helplessness on inmates, rendering them childlike dependents. In addition, they must suffer the indignity of living with each other, that is, with men convicted of murder, rape, robbery, or a winning combination of all three. Such people do not good neighbors make.

Faced with this set of frustrations and deprivations, prisoners seek some kind of solution, eventually settling on a modus vivendi, a code of conduct that promotes unity among them by directing their antagonism toward an enemy, the staff.

1. Don't interfere with inmate interests. Put up a united front against the guards even when this may prove costly to you as an individual.
2. Don't get into arguments, feuds, or grudges with your fellow inmates. Just try to do your time and play it cool.
3. Don't use force, fraud, or other means to exploit your fellow inmates.
4. Be tough and don't whine or weaken. You must learn to put up with a certain amount of frustration. Of course, this does not mean that you should retreat from a fight.
5. As hacks or screws, guards must not be given trust or respect. In any conflict between guards and inmates, the guards are automatically in the wrong.

To be sure, not all inmates live up to these rules or ideals. Some start fights with other inmates for no reason at all, and some take advantage of scarce resources in the prison to sell and buy from inmates who are at a competitive disadvantage. Others enter into homosexual liaisons as the weak partner (punk), or constantly whine and plead their innocence of the crime that brought them into the joint. But a substantial number of inmates are "right guys," who mind their business, keep their promises, remain loyal to their fellow inmates, and otherwise adhere to the inmate code.

The right buy never interferes with other inmates who are conniving against the officials. He doesn't go around looking for a fight, but he never runs away from one when he is in the right. . . . What he's got or can get of the extras in the prison—like cigarettes, food stolen from the mess hall, and so on—he shares with his friends. He doesn't take advantage of those who don't have much. He doesn't strong-arm other inmates into punking or fagging for him; instead, he acts like a man.[4]

This is the deprivation model. Inmates adapt to infuriating prison hardships by banding together and creating an inmate code to reduce the pains of imprisonment. They share and cooperate with each other but refuse to fraternize with the enemy. This strategy allows them to live more comfortably and feel better about themselves: they have created a social order behind bars.

THE REBUTTAL

John Irwin spent five years at Soledad Prison in California, and when he got out he decided to go to college. He was originally bent on majoring in physics, but Donald Cressey convinced him to study prisons instead, and in 1962 they co-authored an article on life inside the joint. In it, Irwin said that the deprivation model did not ring true. In its stead he proposed what has since come to be known as the importation model; this claims that prisoners are not stripped of the identity they had before being incarcerated. Instead, they maintain many of the same norms, values, beliefs, and roles they subscribed to outside the prison environment.

Some inmates had been thieves or sophisticated career criminals in the free world, and in that line of work they learned to be reliable, trustworthy, cool-headed, and "solid" in their everyday dealings with other criminals. They also learned never to give in to the temptation to help the police by providing information. Loyalty and mutual obligation among thieves were their bywords. Once they landed in prison, they retained the same outlook. The convict subculture differed from the thief subculture, for convicts tried to manipulate the prison environment to win special privileges and power over other inmates: stealing, gaining freedom of movement, trying to win status in prison. This orientation was also learned before they got to prison; it was a common variant within lower-class culture.

The thief and convict subcultures differed from each other in important respects, but they had one thing in common: both were interested in maintaining the status quo inside the joint. The convicts were conservative because their schemes and hustles enabled them to make the most of the few resources available inside the prison, to win a few comforts and a certain amount of status. The thieves were conservative because they wished to minimize the troubles and hassles during their stay in prison. They intended to do their own time, avoid tensions and confrontations, and avoid having their sentence extended beyond the minimum. They preferred a peaceful institution.[5]

CHANGE AND CONFLICT

By 1980 Irwin had recanted. He found that neither the deprivation nor the importation model applied any longer. They had been based on the assumption that life behind bars was stable and orderly. That had been true of most prisons in the 1930s, 1940s, and 1950s. But in the 1960s, prisons took on a new look, and the relationships among inmates began to change in ways that would have serious repercussions for all of them. In California and a number of other states outside the South, the old feudal system gave way to a more modern system based on ideas of rehabilitation. Old-line wardens were replaced by new ones who had more education, more sympathy toward inmates, and more faith in their treatment potential.[6]

When correctional institutions replaced the feudal system, they introduced vocational training programs, schooling programs, and group counseling. These helped make the staff and overall environment of the institution more benign and relaxed, which weakened both hostility toward staff members and the inmate code, which was based on such hostility. Inmates tended to think that perhaps some benefits would accrue from participating in these programs; if they did not make them better persons, at least they would help cut down on the time they would have to serve. Programming would get them released sooner. Over the years, these hopes waned, however, as programs failed to deliver as expected, and in some cases sentences grew longer instead of shorter (as originally envisioned in the indeterminate system).

Another source of change came in the form of shifting prison demographics. Inmate population size and composition changed. At one time, prisoners outside the South were predominantly white; blacks, Hispanics, and Native Americans could be found but not in very great numbers. Prisons were segregated; blacks were powerless and handed the most menial jobs. White prisoners were in control, especially right guys, who were numerous enough to have influence. In the 1960s, however, minorities began to fill the prisons, while the proportion of the right guys (or thieves) and sophisticated criminals declined. More and more white inmates came from the rising drug culture.

The vanishing influence of right guys continued the fragmenting of white inmates that had begun when correctional institutions first appeared. Instead of an inmate social system united by a code of some kind, there was a congeries of little cliques. Later, a number of prisons found themselves penetrated by movements from the outside world, stressing black separatism and black nationalism. Black Muslims started the process, and when their influence waned, other groups took over, including the Black Panthers, especially in California. Blacks have been a minority group for hundreds of years, which means that they are socially visible, suffer prejudice and discrimination, and feel self-consciously that they are part of a group. As with any minority, the more they suffer, the stronger their group identification.

The movements stressing soul and nationalism further strengthened the group.[7] Their rising numbers inside the prisons meant that they could do something about their new consciousness; they had something they had never had before: power. In a number of cases blacks took advantage of this by becoming violent. Some inmates became threatening. Others acted by assaulting inmates or guards. And some took to sexual attacks on weaker and smaller whites.

White inmates did not quickly coalesce. They had never had the sense that they were a minority group. They lacked group consciousness. The mere fact that they were white had never been the most prominent factor in their identity; it was taken for granted. No unifying themes such as soul or nationalism could be called upon. Blacks had simply not posed a great enough threat before to make whites think of uniting. But a small group of whites who had always disliked blacks intensely did exist. These bikers or lowriders did band together, at first in some of the western states, to form neo–Nazi groups such as the Aryan Brotherhood. Naturally, their explicitly anti-black stance only heightened tensions within the prisons. The modern prisons became more and more dangerous places.

As tensions mounted so did the prison populations. Today, four million Americans are under some type of correctional supervision. Between 1926 and 1972, the prison population in state and federal facilities grew slowly from about 100,000 to about 200,000. The doubling period lasted 46 years, approximately the same as for the U.S. population then. But from 1972 to 1990, the prison population has increased from 200,000 to 750,000, a doubling period of about ten years. Several explanations for this explosion have been proposed: that judges are putting fewer people on probation than they used to; that more mandatory sentence laws now exist; that arrests for drugs and sexual abuse have risen dramatically; or longer sentences. Also, more people are sentenced for parole violations. It remains to be seen exactly how important each of these factors is.

The increasing number of prisoners was not totally unexpected. Crime was bound to rise as the baby-boom generation reached its late teens. And as they reached their twenties, their criminal records would catch up with the baby boomers and result in prison sentences. Also, the rehabilitative ideal was losing supporters in important circles. Among the most influential thinkers was James Q. Wilson, whose collection of articles *Thinking About Crime*, published in 1975, proposed reducing sentencing discretion and increasing the number of prisoners. When I reviewed the book in 1976, I predicted that his program would "be attended to, because when push comes to shove we all listen to those who anticipated the crisis and have a fairly simple and tough-minded solution."[8] Wilson led the attack against the rehabilitative ideal and advocated imprisonment for its deterrent and incapacitative effects.

If the number of prisoners were to increase greatly, then two consequences followed almost inevitably: (1) many new prisons would have to be built, at great expense to the public treasury, and (2) old prisons would become overcrowded, leading to double bunking, sleeping on cots and floors, and other inconveniences. By 1990, some states found their prisons filled to 200 percent of capacity and under court orders to control the overcrowding or alleviate its more serious ramifications. Prisons and jails were forced to let inmates out sooner than originally scheduled or not let new ones in.

Court orders were something new. In the feudal period, wardens ran their prisons as individual fiefdoms and did not worry much about state legislatures, except for funding, or about state departments of corrections (then nonexistent or insignificant). And they did not worry about the Supreme Court or other courts, because inmates were little more than slaves of the state, and courts maintained a hands-off position, thinking that wardens knew what they were doing and that court officials had no basis for questioning prison policy.

Over the years, prisoners tried to get the courts to intervene. They had little success until the ice was broken by Muslim inmates. These prisoners were regarded by prison administrators as threats to prison order, so when black inmates asked for access to the Muslim newspaper, to the Quran; for the right to hold meetings and the right to bring in Muslim spokesmen; and for segregation and special meals, the administration balked. They would not give in to any of the demands. In the feudal era, they could have gotten away with such a hard line, but not this period, when judicial activism was beginning to appear. Administrators were on particularly weak ground when they denied inmates their religious liberties. That struck the courts as excessive and indefensible; wardens and inmates were on equal footing in the courts (something new and revolutionary), and wardens lost.

In succeeding years, prisoners turned to writ writing with a vengeance. The court was their friend, it seemed. Each year more and more inmates relied on Section 1983 of the Civil Rights Act of 1871, which said that whoever deprives someone else of his or her rights and privileges under the Constitution is liable for damages in a civil suit. Section 1983 helped end the courts' hands-off policy.

This legislation was originally passed with the KKK in mind but has now been used against prison staff. State prisoners file suit in federal court (traditionally more receptive than state courts) when they believe that their freedom of speech, religion, or association has been denied. Also, many of these cases hinge on prison conditions (privacy, sanitation, medical care, food, heating, ventilation, and violence) or due process (in hearings that cover discipline, reclassification, or parole eligibility). Since *Monroe v. Pape* (1961), prisoners have acquired a new status. No longer are they slaves of the states without constitutional rights (though Justices Rehnquist and O'Connor see Section 1983 cases as a waste of time and want a cutback).

The modern prison, like prisons past, has both an authorized and an informal sub rosa economy. The former centers around the canteen or commissary, which inmates can visit periodically to purchase basics, such as cigarettes, toiletries, towels, bedding, and underwear. The sub rosa economy deals in other fare, including food, alcohol, drugs, gambling, prostitution, and weapons. In recent years, there has been a tendency for inmates to conduct their economic transactions only with individuals of their race and for dealing to come under the control of racial gangs. In earlier eras, there was more of an individual entrepreneurial arrangement.

With the increase in prisoners' rights, prisons have opened up more in recent decades. In the process, they have become more permeable, and more goods have been smuggled in by inmates, visitors, and staff members (notably, drugs). Furthermore, inmates nowadays are allowed more money than they once were. No longer do they have to rely on cigarettes to make any kind of transaction. Now real money circulates freely (though it may be contraband in some amounts or in some places, where money is kept locked in an account). The presence of real money inevitably facilitates drug deals. When drugs and money are added to an environment of animosity and violence, the number of untoward incidents rises, because the chances are that many drug deals will go sour. Theft, extortion, blackmail, and robbery have become more pervasive in a number of prisons.

Violence and aggression are one kind of victimization, theft and extortion another, but we should not neglect the third type, variously known as psychological or secondary victimization. Fear, anxiety, and depression cause some inmates to lose sleep and others to become mentally unhinged. Some mutilate themselves. Some try to commit suicide. Jack Henry Abbott, the state-raised youth who wrote *In the Belly of the Beast*, said that in the company of other prisoners, he felt anger, hatred, and paranoia. With constant rage and heightened suspicion of all inmates, he was always ready to go on the attack.[9] Prisons apparently teach many people the value of preemptive strikes.

Conceivably, the pathologies of many of today's prisoners may be related to the stimulus overload. Once upon a time, quietness was strictly enforced. In the days of the penitentiary, the inmates were supposed to be quiet so that they could mediate upon their sinful ways and begin on the path toward redemption. Today, both redemption and quietness are noteworthy mostly by their absence. Loudness is now the order of the day, because of the clanging doors, ear-splitting radios and televisions, and the shouting of stentorian inmates. Aside from the sounds, there are also assaults of another kind, in the form of urine, sweat, and disinfectants. Perhaps the ears could be protected by installing sound-absorbing carpeting, and maybe something could be done for the nose as well. Prison construction, however, has not devoted much thought to either.

Stress can be intolerable for the very old prisoner, or for the newcomer; the inmate from the middle class or a rural area far from the madding crowd; the weak, small, delicate, or apprehensive. To be sure, there are also stresses in the outside world. In those cases, however, a person can escape by quitting the job, severing the marriage, or retreating to some relaxing refuge. Not so in prison, where there are no neighborhood bars, understanding families, or midnight movies. In addition, inmates do not have the option of putting themselves in the care of a professional therapist.

After a while inside, some inmates may find a niche, a microcosm within the prison where they can relax and avoid the noise, threats, and masculinity testing. Niches are spaces where movement in and out is limited, the number of people is small and constant, and the atmosphere is calm and quiet. Often the niche involves a job in the prison (maybe in the kitchen or on the farm, maybe plumbing, carpentry, or operating machinery), but sometimes it involves the inmate's quarters or program (schooling, for instance).

Inmates seek different goals once they have been sent to prison: freedom, safety, privacy, structure, support, emotional feedback, and activity. When they find a subenvironment that suits their tastes and needs, they feel better. They are protected from the annoyances of staff and other inmates, and they learn to live with themselves. In some cases this means that they learn to control their explosive tempers, which may have gotten them in trouble in the first place.

We have been talking about prison inmates, but they are not the only people who occupy the institutions. Guards spend time there, too, and face many of the same problems. They may even be attacked by inmates (though most of the inmate attacks are directed at their fellow prisoners). While guards readily admit that safety is an important worry, they seem more concerned about other matters, notably their lack of power and their inability to control inmates. The many problems confronting guards have been summarized neatly by Hawkins and Alpert in the form of a job description (one not likely to appear in the want ads).

Excellent employment opportunity for men and women who are willing to work eight-hour shifts.... Applicants must enforce numerous rules with few guide-lines. They must be willing to risk physical harm, psychological harassment, and endure the threat of inmate lawsuits.... They must be willing to spend eight hours each day among people who do not like them. They will not be allowed to fraternize with these people, but are expected to control as well as help them. Applicants must accept that they have little or no input into the rules they will be asked to enforce, nor will they be privy to the rationale.... They should realize that management will probably not listen to their complaints.... Promotion is infrequent.... Most of the training will be on the job—often from inmates. All applicants are considered untrustworthy; frequent questioning and searches of private possessions are designed to reduce corruption.[10]

This section gives some indication of what life is like inside contemporary prisons. How much of this picture is conveyed to the reading public by American papers? Do their articles on prisons delve into these matters or largely ignore them and thus leave the public to its own stereotypes?

COVERAGE OF LIFE IN PRISON

To see how well newspapers covered these points, I examined the same 20 papers mentioned in Chapter 8, again for the Monday through Saturday issues during November 1989. Commentators have not written much about how newspapers cover prisons, except that papers say little and tend to cover short-term dramatic events such as large-scale riots. I did not find this to be true of the papers sampled for November 1989. Instead, most papers gave prisons at least a modest amount of coverage and very little of it pertained to rioting.

Prison Population Size and Composition

If the topic of prison population and size includes jail and prison overcrowding, then newspapers mention this topic often. Indeed, they cite it more than any other topic involving prisons. Though articles on prison population appear with considerable frequency, it should not be assumed that they cover the topic with great depth or breadth, for they do not. None of them discussed prison population for the country as a whole, and hardly any discussed the prison population even for that particular state. Moreover, references to prison population in years past are rare and oblique.

A handful of articles, however, did note the fact that the population was rising, and some of these made projections of future populations. According to these articles, states were planning to build more prisons soon, so that the rated capacity could be raised by a few thousand inmates. As one or two reporters said, when those new facilities were ready to admit inmates, however, the state's prison population would again exceed the capacity by a large margin.

The *Cincinnati Enquirer* printed an article that showed some insight into the commonly experienced population problem.

The prison overcrowding problem is even more severe than in jails. Ohio's current prison capacity is 19,748 men and women. The system has about 27,500 inmates, or 139% of capacity.

By 1992, the prison system will be able to hold 21,500 inmates, but by then the inmate population is projected to exceed 33,400 under the current system.

If the legislature, as expected, adopts stiffer penalties for drug offenses, the problem will only worsen, David Dirall, staff director for the panel, noted Friday.[11]

Other articles demonstrated less interest in future population projections and more in the practical problems posed by the present numbers. Many of these stories discussed the new construction that was planned, underway, or just completed. Many also went on to comment on the practice of releasing inmates from jail or prison early. They did not often go into detail on how wardens dealt with the remaining inmates. Articles on double bunking, spreading mattresses on the floor, and similar measures were nonexistent. Perhaps these were seen as having no impact on anyone except the inmates.

While newspapers gave population size an inordinate amount of attention, they did not say much about population composition; only one article dealt with it. In New Mexico, the attorney general proposed more and longer prison sentences for convicted felons because New Mexico's crime problem had reached untenable proportions for such a rural state. In response, a researcher found New Mexico's real problem to be a highly discriminatory sentencing pattern. (To back up this claim, he noted that of those incarcerated during the fiscal year, 52.7 percent were Hispanic, 31.9 percent were "Anglo," 11.7 percent were black, and 3.6 percent

Native American.[12] These figures reveal something about the prison's population composition, but they fail to support the researcher's argument, because they are percentaged in the wrong direction for making causal statements. He would need to say, for each group, what percentage of convicted felons are sent to prison—not what percentage of prisoners belong to each group.)

Inmate Lawsuits and Court Orders

Several articles mentioned court orders, but these were limited to cases involving overcrowding. Other conditions, such as problems with food, time spent inside cells, or the availability of legal or psychological counseling were not brought up in any of the instances where court cases were under discussion. Only a couple of articles took up the issue of lawsuits involving inmates and administration as opposing parties. One of these commented on the case in detail instead of just in passing, so I will quote it at length.

It is not unusual for prison inmates to sue their keepers—for any number of real or unimagined grievances. Occasionally they even win damages.
At the Missouri State Penitentiary, the keepers turned the tables and sued an inmate. And it paid off handsomely for the keepers—$33,000 worth.
An inmate, Rory D. Nitcher, filed suit in federal court against 11 prison officials and corrections officers and the state of Missouri.
Nitcher, a member of a prison white supremacist group known as the Christian Aryan Nation, contended that he was denied full use of the Bible. He also charged that the defendants failed to provide personal hygiene items, such as toothbrush and toothpaste.
The state filed a counterclaim, charging Nitcher with "abuse of process."
Abuse of process is the use of the judicial system for illegal or unwarranted purposes. . . .
The state contended that Nitcher filed the suit—as he had others—for its harassment value and as a means for escape.[13]

The difficulty with this article is that it contains a sample of one (lawsuit). It does not say how many lawsuits inmates file in an average year, nor what fraction of them succeed. When Missouri sued the inmate and won, what did this mean? Was it the only such case to go before the courts? Were there many, and did they often succeed? We have no indication of whether states suing inmates is a new trend, a straw in the wind perhaps, or something far less significant.

The Sub Rosa Economy

As noted, prisons have both a formal and a sub rosa economy. The formal economy is not very exciting, dramatic, or controversial, so we would not expect prison articles to cite it. But two did; each of them dealt with PTL ministers who had been put behind bars for awhile. The newspapers gave Jim Bakker's prison entrance lavish attention, pointing out, for instance, that he would begin working in the kitchen or mopping the floors, for which he would receive 11 to 44 cents an hour. He would be allowed $20 a week in coins for use in the vending machines and could keep from $100 to $150 in a commissary account.

Three articles cited the existence of a sub rosa economy in jails or prisons, though they did not use this term or treat the subject at all broadly. All of them limited the focus to one commodity—drugs. We might expect the subject to be dealt with in large city newspapers such as the *Los Angeles Times*, *Philadelphia Inquirer*, *Detroit News*, or *Washington Post*. Instead, the three articles appeared in papers from the smaller cities, Charleston, South Carolina, Charlotte, North Carolina, and Burlington, Vermont. The paper from little Burlington provided the only detailed article.

According to several inmates interviewed by the *Burlington Free Press*, purchasing and using illegal drugs inside the state's correctional facilities is just about as common as going to the shower—which, coincidentally, is a popular place for smoking marijuana in jail.

Marijuana remains the most common drug in Vermont jails, costing about $3 for a small cigarette, inmates said. But they added that cocaine and Valium are sometimes found within the prison walls. Alcohol is extremely rare because of the difficulty of smuggling it in. . . .

The most common method for smuggling drugs into prison remains "packing"—concealing pouches in the rectum or vagina. The Corrections Department conducts a strip search of virtually every inmate entering prison or returning from visiting hours to detect such smuggling, and brings a physician to the jail for a "body cavity search" if smuggling is suspected.[14]

Violence and Aggression among Inmates

Newspapers do not rush to press with sordid accounts of one inmate victimizing another. Is this because editors have no interest, or because prison officials want it hushed up? Or does the damage that inmates wreak upon each other hold no interest for newspaper readers? To see how the public regards prisoners, I asked my students to write a short description of what they thought life in prison is like. (I do not cover this in class, so the ideas were theirs and not mine.) Some considered prisons pleasant places because of the three meals a day, color television, access to telephones, weekly allowances, exercise equipment, visiting rights, and free housing. The majority, however, likened prisons to a hell hole, where tension, hostility, frustration, and violence were rife while sex, security and privacy were lacking.

Some years ago, I conducted a large survey in the state of Washington to measure attitudes and opinions regarding crime and the criminal justice system. One part of the sixteen-page questionnaire dealt with prison conditions for inmates. I wanted to determine how citizens thought prisoners should be treated—harshly or humanely. The consensus then among prison officials was that the public had no stomach for prison reform, that it did not have any desire to see inmates receive the "benefits" of ordinary living conditions. But the results of this survey and a few others indicated otherwise, for most citizens said cells should be provided with plenty of room, light, heat, and ventilation; inmates should be allowed to make formal complaints to the courts about prison conditions; and violent offenders should be closely supervised to prevent them from attacking other inmates.

It might be stretching matters a bit to conclude that these results mean there are vast wellsprings of sympathy for prisoners, but it does seem that the public tends to think of them as human beings who deserve certain rights and protections. Thus it may be that public apathy is not the reason for so little news of prison victimization. Maybe the fault lies with prison administrators or newspaper editors. Maybe they consider inmates several notches below human and thus undeserving of news coverage.

Newspapers did not maintain a complete blackout of inmate-on-inmate violence; three items slipped through the iron curtain. In one story, a man in jail for a traffic offense was put in the same cell as a murderer, who threatened to kill him if he did not perform oral sex. He refused and received a harsh beating for it. In another case, two Hispanics drugged and raped a black inmate. In the third incident, a reputed Junior Black Mafia street boss stabbed an inmate in the face and back a number of times. Once in court, the victim, fearing reprisal, professed sudden amnesia about the incident, saying that he never got a look at his assailant. Such incidents may take place frequently but do not make the newspapers unless they become court cases—which happens only in rare instances.

Noise, Odors, Psychological Victimization

In general, these drew minimal coverage. One article did go into some detail about Larry Spotted Blanket, whose habits of hygiene endeared him neither to guards nor to other inmates. Disdaining the toilet, he relieved himself in the cell and smeared the results over the cell walls. Whenever he was to be jailed, guards would call in sick. Other articles dealt with suicides of inmates but did not probe the causes. In addition, newspaper articles on prison life scarcely noticed or mentioned the existence of niches or sanctuaries where inmates can relax and eke out a measure of safety and satisfaction. Probably few reporters have any familiarity with the concept.

Guards

In the old days, corrections staff members were called guards by those who thought well of them and cops, screws, or hacks by those who did not. It seems that reporters also think of them as cops, though in a much different sense. Reporters consider them to be worthy individuals, for the most part, because they work at an occupation society considers crucial and thus deserve public appreciation for their efforts. This means that when inmates attack or kidnap guards, reporters write about it as a heinous offense that should be regarded by the rest of society as intolerable.

When corrections staff do something just as flagrant to inmates, this fact has little chance of becoming public. If there is some official action taken, however, the media may seize upon the event and magnify its seriousness. In the back of reporters' minds may lurk the old stereotype of guards as brutal and sadistic. A few stories involved staff members as victims of violence, a few more depicted them as perpetrators of violence, and several of the latter told of staff forcing sex upon female inmates. Some stories detailed the low pay and lower morale among guards and the resultant difficulty in recruiting more of them.

CONCLUSION

Commentators say little about media coverage of prisons except that there is too little of it and what there is dwells on riots and escapes at the expense of stories on what life is like behind bars. James Jacobs found these criticisms unsubstantiated in his media study of 1976. And also in this chapter these claims proved inaccurate. In the 20 papers examined here, prisons did not receive as much coverage as the courts, but they got as much coverage as could be reasonably expected. Moreover, most of the news on prisons did not deal with riots—almost none did, although riots did take place at the time. (At Camp Hill, Pennsylvania, for instance, so many buildings were burned that prisoners had to be dispersed throughout the United States.)

If newspapers were examined a few years ago, the coverage might have been less extensive and less insightful. But prisons have made the news in recent years because crowding and financial pressures have pushed them into the political and economic arenas. It is news when society runs out of space and starts diverting its unwanted to tin sheds, tents, barges, mess halls, and military bases. It is also news when new jails and prisons are built or planned. The usual response to them is "not in my backyard."

Newspapers may take a more sociological approach to prisons than to courts. Prison stories lend themselves to discussion of the entire institution instead of one particular inmate or one particular case. Prisons are long-term residences with large collections of inmates. Courts do not have this long-term or collective nature. Therefore, newspaper articles do not usually try to treat the courts as institutions. From a sociological point of view, prison articles in recent years have become more informative than articles on the courts.

The fact remains that prisons are remote institutions, about which most Americans are woefully ignorant. It is easy to blame newspapers for this state of affairs, and for many years that would have been appropriate. Newspapers were not doing the job, nor were any of the other media. But in the past couple of years, the prison has come out from behind the iron curtain, and some newspapers are reporting on them in a way that is more informative than critics have intimated. Newspaper coverage may not be very good, but I would not give it an F.

NOTES

1. James Jacobs, *New Perspectives on Prisons and Imprisonment* (Ithaca, NY: Cornell University Press, 1983), pp. 106–112.

2. Richard Ericson, Patricia Baranek, and Janet Chin, *Negotiating Control* (Toronto: University of Toronto Press, 1989), p. 11.

3. Donald Clemmer, *The Prison Community* (New York: Rinehart, 1958).

4. Gresham Sykes and Sheldon Messinger, "Inmate Social System," in *Crime and Justice*, vol. 3, ed. Sir Leon Radzinowicz and Marvin Wolfgang (New York: Basic Books, 1977), p. 187.

5. John Irwin and Donald Cressey, "Thieves, Convicts and the Inmate Culture," *Social Problems* 10 (Fall 1962): 142–155.

6. John Irwin, *Prisons in Turmoil* (Boston: Little, Brown, 1980).

7. Ibid.

8. Roy Lotz, "Symposium on Wilson's Thinking About Crime," *Contemporary Sociology* 5 (July 1976): 412.

9. Jack Henry Abbott, *In the Belly of the Beast* (New York: Vintage, 1982).

10. Richard Hawkins and Geoffrey Alpert, *American Prison Systems* (Englewood Cliffs, NJ: Prentice-Hall, 1989), p. 338.

11. Dick Kimmins, "Release Nonviolent Inmates Early, Panel Says," *Cincinnati Enquirer*, November 20, 1989, p. E–2.

12. Doug McClellan, "Expert Says Sentencing Disproportional in New Mexico," *Albuquerque Journal*, November 29, 1989, p. A1.

13. John Dauner, "Inmate's Lawsuit Against State Backfires," *Kansas City Times*, November 10, 1989, p. B–2.

14. James Bressor, "Drugs Rampant in Vermont State Prisons," *Burlington Free Press*, November 27, 1989, p. 4A.

Chapter Ten

The Critics

THE NEW PESSIMISM

In the early to mid–1980s, industry experts cited newspapers as a thriving business.[1] But discussion took on a much different tone in later years; according to the new consensus, the newspapers were in trouble. The National Opinion Research Center asked people in 1967 how often they read a paper, and 73 percent said every day. But by 1989 daily readers plummeted to 50 percent—and only half that among people aged 18 to 29 (and even those tended to read selectively, perhaps only the comics, classified, and television sections).[2]

Commentators on the business side note that while the adult population in America has grown considerably in the past 20 years or so, newspaper circulation has not. Instead, it has stagnated. Thus, household penetration has fallen off quite noticeably. Nowadays there are 64 newspapers sold for every 100 households in America, as opposed to 99 per 100 back in 1970.[3] Those aware of this shrinking penetration have speculated about its cause, naturally, and among their suggestions, perhaps the most common idea is that today's papers tend toward the dull, drab, boring, and colorless.

If the steep decline in household penetration generated gloomy articles, so did slumps in company profits, news budgets, and newspaper advertising.[4] Some observers became apocalyptic, foreseeing the elimination of newspapers. One said that there is a beginning, middle, and end to everything, and at least newspapers can take heart in the fact that they have enjoyed such a long run. Another imagined being a grandfather one day and reminiscing about the olden days when things such as newspapers still existed. A Knight-Ridder executive conceded that the demise of printed papers was inevitable, regardless of what steps the industry might take to prevent it.[5]

Several commentators declared newspapers dinosaurs, relics that failed to evolve and thus drifted out of touch with young people and minorities. They became irrelevant largely because of their owners and editors, who tend overwhelmingly to be white, middle-aged, and middle-class males. They pitch their product to the kind of people they know best, which is to say, white, middle-aged, and middle-class readers. According to these analysts, newspapers in the present era are faltering because they hold no excitement for potential readers.

What may be the most interesting aspect of this line of argument (the hand wringing and doomsaying) is how it relates to the usual litany of criticisms directed at the media over the past two or three decades: that they are too powerful, too sensational, and too leftist. If the National Opinion Research Center's findings are to be believed (and there is no reason to doubt them), then readers are leaving the papers in droves or (at best) coming to them in dribbles. If this is the case, then it would appear that the medium is not the powerful and influential force earlier critics assumed. If papers are dull, drab, and colorless, it is nonsensical to criticize them for sensationalism and overdramatizing. If they are the stodgy products of old, unimaginative white men and meant for similar kinds of readers, it hardly seems likely that they would slant their news articles in a very radical direction (since most white suburban readers vote Republican).

Nevertheless, conservative commentators insist that newspapers usually take a leftist line: not sufficiently respectful of conventional values and not sufficiently objective when reporting on political issues. For instance, a political official in Pennsylvania said not long ago that the major purveyors of news glamorize America's enemies, undercut our elected leaders, and always blame America first. "It is time we leveled at them the same criticism they have lavished upon society as a whole."[6]

Actually, it is clear that they have leveled it. As Russell Baker notes, "The American press is a wonderful target right now for both criticism and constructive abuse."[7] Scores of books have appeared in recent years setting forth the press's faults, and magazine articles have done the same. To measure the latter, we need only consult the *Reader's Guide to Periodical Literature* and look under the heading of journalistic ethics. (These articles criticize the media for lacking them.) There were none until the period between March 1959 and February 1961, when three articles appeared. The high point was reached in 1981, when there were 48 articles. Throughout the 1980s, there were 20 or more articles almost every year. The best known, which appeared in *Time*, said that reporters are perceived as ogreish, for they are rude and accusatory, cynical and unpatriotic. They twist facts to suit their not-so-hidden liberal agenda. They meddle in politics, and then walk off without regard to the pain and chaos they leave behind. They are arrogant and self-righteous, brushing aside most criticism as the uninformed carping of cranks and ideologues. To top it off, they claim that their behavior is sanctioned, indeed sanctified, by the U.S. Constitution.[8]

It is perhaps understandable that someone would eventually do a broad analysis of the many media critics. Two interesting works along this line have been done by Joli Jensen and Steven Starker. Independently, they seem to have come upon the same metaphor for their analysis. Jensen says that it is the updated story of the serpent, Eve, and the Garden of Eden. The media are the powerful, seductive, and corrupting element in this morality tale. Starker too talks about evil influences (that is the name of his book). He says that the media are charged with threatening the character and morality of youths and adults and the American way of life by stimulating crime and violence, undermining sexual mores and legitimate authority, manipulating consumers, promoting materialism, and substituting fantasy for reality. He adds that "the idea that a single source of evil influence is the key to understanding much of human behavior perhaps derives from America's Puritan religious heritage."[9]

EARLIER YEARS

The Starker and Jensen analyses attribute media criticism to a reawakened Puritanism, a religious fervor that identifies the media as a modern-day Satan and thus a convenient scapegoat for a host of problems, social and psychological. What these analyses do not explain, though, is the peculiar timing of this moral rearmament. Why should criticism of journalism reach its peak in the 1980s instead of, say, the 1940s or 1950s? Is it because in those earlier decades newspapers were so much better that criticism would have been inappropriate?

Not according to most of the experts in the field. For instance, David Shaw concludes that newspapers of today, at least in America, are more accurate, impartial, and comprehensive than newspapers were at any other time in their history. Everette Dennis seems to agree with this assessment, particularly in the realm of public-affairs reporting. And so do Merrill and Fisher. In *The World's Greatest Dailies*, they conclude that elite newspapers are getting better all the time, by which they mean providing more serious discussion and responsible interpretation, more accuracy and balance. Finally, according to Lloyd Tataryn, the present generation of reporters is more educated, more idea conscious, more politically aware, and more socially concerned than reporters of past decades.[10]

Reporters have changed over the years. A long-time veteran of Philadelphia papers says that in the old days, many reporters carried a flask and had long spells when they were too drunk to move, let alone report. They also developed close ties with police and politicians, which prevented them from reporting the fact that these people were looting the city.[11] Rodney Smolla says that in earlier decades, journalism was a seedier business, and readers knew enough to take the news with a grain of salt. Reporters were raffish fellows who dressed in rumpled suits, drank heavily, and received little pay. In those days, "reporting was surely much worse than it is today, but it was also less harmful, because there was no presumption or pretension of accuracy."[12]

At home, newspapers were apt to pen fearless editorials lauding retiring fire chiefs who had managed to go years without falling off a ladder.[13] Newspapers provided cheer and comfort, jingoism and conventional wisdom. They imagined little corruption in capitalist societies and almost nothing commendable or successful in socialist ones. In foreign affairs, American reporters usually wrote what was conveyed to them in carefully staged briefings. Not all of these habits had died by the 1960s, either, for after studying 1,800 articles in six newspapers, Clarence Wyatt concluded that the press in Vietnam relied on official information and reported that information with only an occasional qualification.[14]

Some of the newspapers now held in highest esteem were quite awful back in the 1950s and earlier. The *Los Angeles Times*, *Chicago Tribune*, and *Philadelphia Inquirer* may be taken as examples of this transformation. In Los Angeles the *Times* did not mention Democrats. It was as if they had dropped off the face of the earth. The front page did mention other things, however, providing complete rosters of local football teams each Saturday and an incredible number of stories on the local weather, even when it was in no way exceptional. Perhaps this meteorological obsession was an attempt to lure people from less salubrious climates to southern California.

On the front page, a reader would also find more than a few stories about movie stars and lesser lights of the entertainment industry. One day there were four such stories on the front page, one each on Bob Hope, Elizabeth Taylor, Jonathan Winters, and the now-forgotten Linda Christian. Stories about train, plane, and car crashes were abundant. And so were gushing accounts of local trivia, such as parades.

It was a daydream day for the world's greatest floral spectacle with its 1958 theme of "Daydreams in Flowers."

Only a few white clouds feathered the warm blue sky.

In the soft brilliant air the billion flowers of the floats glittered like colored suns.

The crowds massed solid along the line of march were warm and cheerful and pleased.

The trees stood silent in the still sky. . . .

The setting was flawless.

And the parade did it justice.

Southern California's bottomless cornucopia poured out its annual crop of dazzling flowers and dazzling girls.[15]

The *Chicago Tribune* was hardly an improvement. In 1954 its favorite word was "Red" and its favorite person Joe McCarthy, so that any political article was likely to turn into a diatribe against the pinkoes or a celebration of those professing to protect America from them.

The Republican party, born 100 years ago to combat slavery, today was rededicated to the ideal of freedom in this city [Jackson, Michigan] where its first state convention was held. . . .

Vice President Nixon, principal speaker, emphasized that the struggle between the forces of freedom and slavery today is worldwide. Nevertheless, he agreed with the contention of Abraham Lincoln, more than a hundred years ago, and of Senator McCarthy today, that internal subversion, rather than war, is the greatest danger confronting the United States.[16]

If a paper can liken McCarthy to Lincoln, then it clearly recognizes no limits to its zeal.

In the *Philadelphia Inquirer* of the 1950s, there was a different pattern of news produced. It did not go in for as much Red baiting as the Chandlers of the *Los Angeles Times* or Colonel McCormick of the *Chicago Tribune*. Nor did it display as much antagonism toward labor. Its main claim to fame was a fondness for snippets, items one or two paragraphs long. The front page provided 20 or 30 of these (instead of six or seven long articles) and thus provided readers with a collage of fragments each day. Saturated with evanescent tidbits, readers must have supposed that nothing serious in the world was happening.

Apparently oblivious or acquiescent, critics then offered no scathing denunciations, though many newspapers warranted them. News in the 1950s was sometimes a weary apologia for conservatism and cold warriorism, sometimes frivolous and distracting minutiae. The bleak condition of journalism then could have been deftly skewered by critics and it would not have required a very strenuous effort, but critics winked at the condition (according to the *Readers Guide*) and the press escaped with almost no bad reviews.

The same cannot be said of journalism today, for critics have risen like a chorus to insist there is something rotten in the press of ours. This is quite incongruous, because it comes at a time when, by more objective reading, the press has improved greatly over the recent past. Equally baffling, critics have hounded the most serious and impressive papers, such as the *Washington Post* and *New York Times*. Sometimes these papers do go astray (as when the *Times* tries to cover student uprisings) but often criticism reveals more about the critic than what he or she is criticizing.

What is the best way to express this situation, this tendency of critics to pounce on the best and brightest newspapers while ignoring the manifest shortcomings of the worst? Someone with a Biblical way of speaking might say of such critics that they now strain at a gnat though once they would swallow a camel. And why do they now criticize so freely? Perhaps there has been a revolution of rising expectations in the world of newspapers, and critics' standards continue to soar ever higher, beyond what it is reasonable to expect newspaper articles to reach. Maybe such criticism is not harmful, but it does show a lack of balance or proportion. Those the Bible said strained at a gnat but swallowed a camel were called "blind guides." Maybe that description applies to today's critics.

NOTES

1. Leo Bogart, "Newspapers in Transition," *The Wilson Quarterly* 6 (Special Issue 1982): 58–70; Lawrence Lichty, "Video Versus Print," *The Wilson Quarterly* 6 (Special Issue 1982): 48–57.

2. Gerald Stone, "Recent Research About Young Readers and Newspapers," paper presented at the 1990 American Newspaper Publishers Association Conference; Robert Samuelson, "Does Anyone Read Anymore?" *Washington Post*, May 2, 1990, p. A23.

3. Alex Jones, "Papers Urged to Include Minorities," *New York Times*, April 25, 1990, p. D23.

4. George Garneau, "Double-Digit Declines," *Editor and Publisher* 123 (May 12, 1990): 14–16; Patricia Chisolm, "Losses For Words," *Maclean's* 103 (May 14, 1990): 42–44; Janet Meyers, "Gloomy Forecast," *Advertising Age* 61 (April 16, 1990): 70; Alex Jones, "Newspaper Executives See Falling Profits," *New York Times*, April 27, 1990, p. D18; Mark Fitzgerald, "A Challenging Year," *Editor and Publisher* 123 (January 6, 1990): 11–13, 46–47.

5. Donald Katz, "Are Newspapers Yesterday's News?" *Esquire* 113 (January 1990): 39–40.

6. Richard Snyder, "Can We Trust the Big Media?" *Vital Speeches* 51 (January 1, 1985): 174.

7. Richard Clurman, *Beyond Malice* (New Brunswick, NJ: Transaction, 1988), p. 21.

8. William Henry III, "Journalism Under Fire," *Time* 122 (December 12, 1983): 76.

9. Steven Starker, *Evil Influences* (New Brunswick, NJ: Transaction, 1989), p. 6; Joli Jensen, *Redeeming Modernity* (Newbury Park, CA: Sage, 1990).

10. David Shaw, *Press Watch* (New York: Macmillan, 1984); Everette Dennis,

Reshaping the Media (Newbury Park, CA: Sage, 1989); John Merrill and Harold Fisher, *The World's Great Dailies* (New York: Hastings House, 1980); Lloyd Tataryn, *The Pundits* (Toronto: Deneau, 1985).

11. "Seven Voices," *Columbia Journalism Review* 23 (November 1986): 49–64.

12. Rodney Smolla, *Suing the Press* (New York: Oxford University Press, 1986), p. 11.

13. Ben Bagdikian, *The Effete Conspiracy* (New York: Harper and Row, 1972), p. 3.

14. Clarence Wyatt, " 'At the Cannon's Mouth': The American Press and the Vietnam War," *Journalism History* 13 (Autumn 1986): 111.

15. Jack Smith, "Rose Parade Delights Huge Throng," *Los Angeles Times*, January 2, 1958, p. 1.

16. Chesly Manly, "Republicans Rededicated to Old Ideals," *Chicago Tribune*, July 7, 1954, p. 1.

Selected Bibliography

Black, Jay, and Frederick Whitney. *Introduction to Mass Communication*. Dubuque, IA: William C. Brown, 1988.

Bogart, Leo. *The Press and the Public*. Hillsdale, NJ: Erlbaum, 1989.

Chibnall, Steve. *Law and Order News*. London: Tavistock, 1977.

Conklin, John. *The Impact of Crime*. New York: Macmillan, 1975.

DeFleur, Melvin, and Sandra Ball-Rokeach. *Theories of Mass Communication*. New York: Longman, 1982.

Drechsel, Robert. *News Making in the Trial Courts*. New York: Longman, 1983.

Ericson, Richard, Patricia Baranek, and Janet Chin. *Negotiating Control*. Toronto: University of Toronto Press, 1989.

———. *Visualizing Deviance*. Toronto: University of Toronto Press, 1987.

Fishman, Mark. *Manufacturing the News*. Austin: University of Texas Press, 1980.

Gans, Herbert. *Deciding What's News*. New York: Vintage, 1980.

Gerbner, George, and Larry Gross. "The Scary World of TV's Heavy Viewer." *Psychology Today* 9 (1976): 41–45, 89.

Graber, Doris. *Crime News and the Public*. New York: Praeger, 1980.

Halberstam, David. *The Powers That Be*. New York: Dell, 1979.

Heath, Linda. "Impact of Newspaper Crime Reports on Fear of Crime." *Journal of Personality and Social Psychology* 47 (1984): 263–276.

Hiebert, Ray, and Carol Reuss. *Impact of Mass Media*. New York: Longman, 1988.

Hirsch, Paul. "The 'Scary World' of the Nonviewer and Other Anomalies." *Communications Research* 7 (1980): 403–456.

Humphries, Drew. "Serious Crime, News Coverage and Ideology." *Crime and Delinquency* 27 (1981): 191–205.

Klapper, Joseph. *The Effects of Mass Communication*. Glencoe, IL: Free Press, 1960.

Lazarsfeld, Paul, Bernard Berelson, and Hazel Gaudet. *The People's Choice*. New York: Columbia University Press, 1948.

Lichter, Robert, Stanley Rothman, and Linda Lichter. *The Media Elite*. Bethesda, MD: Adler and Adler, 1986.

Lowery, Shearon, and Melvin DeFleur. *Milestones in Mass Communication Research*. New York: Longman, 1988.

Manoff, Robert, and Michael Schudson. *Reading the News*. New York: Pantheon, 1987.

Roshco, Bernard. *Newsmaking*. Chicago: University of Chicago Press, 1975.

Schudson, Michael. *Discovering the News*. New York: Basic Books, 1978.

Shaw, David. *Press Watch*. New York: Macmillan, 1984.

Stark, Rodney. *Sociology*. Belmont, CA: Wadsworth, 1989.

Stephens, Mitchell. *A History of News*. New York: Viking, 1988.

————. "Crime Doesn't Pay: Except on the Newsstands." *Washington Journalism Review* 3 (1981): 39–43.

Swanberg, W. A. *Citizen Hearst*. New York: Scribner's, 1961.

————. *Pulitzer*. New York: Scribner's, 1967.

Tuchman, Gaye. *Making News*. New York: Free Press, 1978.

Williams, Tannis. *The Impact of Television*. Orlando, Academic Press, 1986.

Winick, Charles. *Deviance and Mass Media*. Beverly Hills, CA: Sage, 1978.

Index

ABOUT THE AUTHOR

ROY EDWARD LOTZ is an associate professor of sociology at John Jay College of Criminal Justice in New York City; this is one of many colleges in the City University system. Previously, he spent several years on the sociology faculty at Washington State University, which then housed mass communication stalwarts Milton Rokeach, Melvin DeFleur, and Sandra Ball-Rokeach and delinquency scholars James F. Short, Jr. and Ivan Nye. He has published widely on crime, delinquency, and a variety of other topics.